HBR'S 10 MUST READS

On
Leadership

On
Leadership

HARVARD BUSINESS REVIEW PRESS
Boston, Massachusetts

No part of this publication may be reproduced, stored in or introduced into a retrieval system, or transmitted, in any form, or by any means (electronic, mechanical, photocopying, recording, or otherwise), without the prior permission of the publisher. Requests for permission should be directed to permissions@hbsp.harvard.edu, or mailed to Permissions, Harvard Business School Publishing, 60 Harvard Way, Boston, Massachusetts 02163.

Library of Congress Cataloging-in-Publication Data
HBR's 10 must reads on leadership
    p. cm.
  Includes index.
  ISBN 978-1-4221-5797-8 (pbk. : alk. paper) 1. Leadership. I. Harvard
business review. II. Title: HBR's ten must reads on leadership.
III. Title: Harvard business review's 10 must reads on leadership.
  HD57.7.H3914 2010
  658.4'092—dc22

                                                        2010031617

The paper used in this publication meets the requirements of the American National Standard for Permanence of Paper for Publications and Documents in Libraries and Archives Z39.48-1992.

Contents

On
Leadership

What Makes a Leader?

by Daniel Goleman

EVERY BUSINESSPERSON KNOWS a story about a highly intelligent, highly skilled executive who was promoted into a leadership position only to fail at the job. And they also know a story about someone with solid—but not extraordinary—intellectual abilities and technical skills who was promoted into a similar position and then soared.

Such anecdotes support the widespread belief that identifying individuals with the "right stuff" to be leaders is more art than science. After all, the personal styles of superb leaders vary: Some leaders are subdued and analytical; others shout their manifestos from the mountaintops. And just as important, different situations call for different types of leadership. Most mergers need a sensitive negotiator at the helm, whereas many turnarounds require a more forceful authority.

I have found, however, that the most effective leaders are alike in one crucial way: They all have a high degree of what has come to be known as *emotional intelligence*. It's not that IQ and technical skills are irrelevant. They do matter, but mainly as "threshold capabilities"; that is, they are the entry-level requirements for executive positions. But my research, along with other recent studies, clearly shows that emotional intelligence is the sine qua non of leadership. Without it, a person can have the best training in the world, an incisive, analytical mind, and an endless supply of smart ideas, but he still won't make a great leader.

In the course of the past year, my colleagues and I have focused on how emotional intelligence operates at work. We have examined the relationship between emotional intelligence and effective performance, especially in leaders. And we have observed how emotional intelligence shows itself on the job. How can you tell if someone has high emotional intelligence, for example, and how can you recognize it in yourself? In the following pages, we'll explore these questions, taking each of the components of emotional intelligence—self-awareness, self-regulation, motivation, empathy, and social skill—in turn.

Evaluating Emotional Intelligence

Most large companies today have employed trained psychologists to develop what are known as "competency models" to aid them in identifying, training, and promoting likely stars in the leadership firmament. The psychologists have also developed such models for lower-level positions. And in recent years, I have analyzed competency models from 188 companies, most of which were large and global and included the likes of Lucent Technologies, British Airways, and Credit Suisse.

In carrying out this work, my objective was to determine which personal capabilities drove outstanding performance within these organizations, and to what degree they did so. I grouped capabilities into three categories: purely technical skills like accounting and business planning; cognitive abilities like analytical reasoning; and competencies demonstrating emotional intelligence, such as the ability to work with others and effectiveness in leading change.

To create some of the competency models, psychologists asked senior managers at the companies to identify the capabilities that typified the organization's most outstanding leaders. To create other models, the psychologists used objective criteria, such as a division's profitability, to differentiate the star performers at senior levels within their organizations from the average ones. Those

Idea in Brief

What distinguishes great leaders from merely good ones? It isn't IQ or technical skills, says Daniel Goleman. It's **emotional intelligence**: a group of five skills that enable the best leaders to maximize their own *and* their followers' performance. When senior managers at one company had a critical mass of EI capabilities, their divisions outperformed yearly earnings goals by 20%.

The EI skills are:

- *Self-awareness*—knowing one's strengths, weaknesses, drives, values, and impact on others

- *Self-regulation*—controlling or redirecting disruptive impulses and moods

- *Motivation*—relishing achievement for its own sake

- *Empathy*—understanding other people's emotional makeup

- *Social skill*—building rapport with others to move them in desired directions

We're each born with certain levels of EI skills. But we can strengthen these abilities through persistence, practice, and feedback from colleagues or coaches.

individuals were then extensively interviewed and tested, and their capabilities were compared. This process resulted in the creation of lists of ingredients for highly effective leaders. The lists ranged in length from seven to 15 items and included such ingredients as initiative and strategic vision.

When I analyzed all this data, I found dramatic results. To be sure, intellect was a driver of outstanding performance. Cognitive skills such as big-picture thinking and long-term vision were particularly important. But when I calculated the ratio of technical skills, IQ, and emotional intelligence as ingredients of excellent performance, emotional intelligence proved to be twice as important as the others for jobs at all levels.

Moreover, my analysis showed that emotional intelligence played an increasingly important role at the highest levels of the company, where differences in technical skills are of negligible importance. In other words, the higher the rank of a person considered to be a star performer, the more emotional intelligence capabilities showed up as the reason for his or her effectiveness. When I compared star performers with average ones in senior leadership positions, nearly

Idea in Practice

Understanding EI'S Components

EI Component	Definition	Hallmarks	Example
Self-awareness	Knowing one's emotions, strengths, weaknesses, drives, values, and goals—and their impact on others	• Self-confidence • Realistic self-assessment • Self-deprecating sense of humor • Thirst for constructive criticism	A manager knows tight deadlines bring out the worst in him. So he plans his time to get work done well in advance.
Self-regulation	Controlling or redirecting disruptive emotions and impulses	• Trustworthiness • Integrity • Comfort with ambiguity and change	When a team botches a presentation, its leader resists the urge to scream. Instead, she considers possible reasons for the failure, explains the consequences to her team, and explores solutions with them.
Motivation	Being driven to achieve for the sake of achievement	• A passion for the work itself and for new challenges • Unflagging energy to improve • Optimism in the face of failure	A portfolio manager at an investment company sees his fund tumble for three consecutive quarters. Major clients defect. Instead of blaming external circumstances, she decides to learn from the experience—and engineers a turnaround.

Empathy	Considering others' feelings, especially when making decisions	• Expertise in attracting and retaining talent • Ability to develop others • Sensitivity to cross-cultural differences	An American consultant and her team pitch a project to a potential client in Japan. Her team interprets the client's silence as disapproval, and prepares to leave. The consultant reads the client's body language and senses interest. She continues the meeting, and her team gets the job.
Social Skill	Managing relationships to move people in desired directions	• Effectiveness in leading change • Persuasiveness • Extensive networking • Expertise in building and leading teams	A manager wants his company to adopt a better Internet strategy. He finds kindred spirits and assembles a de facto team to create a prototype Web site. He persuades allies in other divisions to fund the company's participation in a relevant convention. His company forms an Internet division—and puts him in charge of it.

Strengthening Your EI

Use practice and feedback from others to strengthen specific EI skills.

Example: An executive learned from others that she lacked empathy, especially the ability to listen. She wanted to fix the problem, so she asked a coach to tell her when she exhibited poor listening skills. She then role-played incidents to practice giving better responses; for example, not interrupting. She also began observing executives skilled at listening—and imitated their behavior.

The five components of emotional intelligence at work

	Definition	Hallmarks
Self-awareness	The ability to recognize and understand your moods, emotions, and drives, as well as their effect on others	Self-confidence Realistic self-assessment Self-deprecating sense of humor
Self-Regulation	The ability to control or redirect disruptive impulses and moods The propensity to suspend judgment—to think before acting	Trustworthiness and integrity Comfort with ambiguity Openness to change
Motivation	A passion to work for reasons that go beyond money or status A propensity to pursue goals with energy and persistence	Strong drive to achieve Optimism, even in the face of failure Organizational commitment
Empathy	The ability to understand the emotional makeup of other people Skill in treating people according to their emotional reactions	Expertise in building and retaining talent Cross-cultural sensitivity Service to clients and customers
Social Skill	Proficiency in managing relationships and building networks An ability to find common ground and build rapport	Effectiveness in leading change Persuasiveness Expertise in building and leading teams

90% of the difference in their profiles was attributable to emotional intelligence factors rather than cognitive abilities.

Other researchers have confirmed that emotional intelligence not only distinguishes outstanding leaders but can also be linked to strong performance. The findings of the late David McClelland, the renowned researcher in human and organizational behavior, are a good example. In a 1996 study of a global food and beverage company, McClelland found that when senior managers had a critical mass of emotional intelligence capabilities, their divisions outperformed yearly earnings goals by 20%. Meanwhile, division leaders without that critical mass underperformed by almost the same amount. McClelland's findings, interestingly, held as true in the company's U.S. divisions as in its divisions in Asia and Europe.

In short, the numbers are beginning to tell us a persuasive story about the link between a company's success and the emotional intelligence of its leaders. And just as important, research is also demonstrating that people can, if they take the right approach, develop their emotional intelligence. (See the sidebar "Can Emotional Intelligence Be Learned?")

Self-Awareness

Self-awareness is the first component of emotional intelligence—which makes sense when one considers that the Delphic oracle gave the advice to "know thyself" thousands of years ago. Self-awareness means having a deep understanding of one's emotions, strengths, weaknesses, needs, and drives. People with strong self-awareness are neither overly critical nor unrealistically hopeful. Rather, they are honest—with themselves and with others.

People who have a high degree of self-awareness recognize how their feelings affect them, other people, and their job performance. Thus, a self-aware person who knows that tight deadlines bring out the worst in him plans his time carefully and gets his work done well in advance. Another person with high self-awareness will be able to work with a demanding client. She will understand the client's impact on her moods and the deeper reasons for her frustration. "Their

Can Emotional Intelligence Be Learned?

FOR AGES, PEOPLE HAVE DEBATED if leaders are born or made. So too goes the debate about emotional intelligence. Are people born with certain levels of empathy, for example, or do they acquire empathy as a result of life's experiences? The answer is both. Scientific inquiry strongly suggests that there is a genetic component to emotional intelligence. Psychological and developmental research indicates that nurture plays a role as well. How much of each perhaps will never be known, but research and practice clearly demonstrate that emotional intelligence can be learned.

One thing is certain: Emotional intelligence increases with age. There is an old-fashioned word for the phenomenon: maturity. Yet even with maturity, some people still need training to enhance their emotional intelligence. Unfortunately, far too many training programs that intend to build leadership skills—including emotional intelligence—are a waste of time and money. The problem is simple: They focus on the wrong part of the brain.

Emotional intelligence is born largely in the neurotransmitters of the brain's limbic system, which governs feelings, impulses, and drives. Research indicates that the limbic system learns best through motivation, extended practice, and feedback. Compare this with the kind of learning that goes on in the neocortex, which governs analytical and technical ability. The neocortex grasps concepts and logic. It is the part of the brain that figures out how to use a computer or make a sales call by reading a book. Not surprisingly—but mistakenly—it is also the part of the brain targeted by most training programs aimed at enhancing emotional intelligence. When such programs take, in effect, a neocortical approach, my research with the Consortium for Research on Emotional Intelligence in Organizations has shown they can even have a *negative* impact on people's job performance.

To enhance emotional intelligence, organizations must refocus their training to include the limbic system. They must help people break old behavioral habits and establish new ones. That not only takes much more time than conventional training programs, it also requires an individualized approach.

Imagine an executive who is thought to be low on empathy by her colleagues. Part of that deficit shows itself as an inability to listen; she interrupts people and doesn't pay close attention to what they're saying. To fix the problem, the executive needs to be motivated to change, and then she needs practice and feedback from others in the company. A colleague or coach could be tapped to let the executive know when she has been observed failing to listen. She would then have to replay the incident and give a better response; that is, demonstrate her ability to absorb what others are saying. And the executive could be directed to observe certain executives who listen well and to mimic their behavior.

With persistence and practice, such a process can lead to lasting results. I know one Wall Street executive who sought to improve his empathy—specifically his ability to read people's reactions and see their perspectives. Before beginning his quest, the executive's subordinates were terrified of working with him. People even went so far as to hide bad news from him. Naturally, he was shocked when finally confronted with these facts. He went home and told his family—but they only confirmed what he had heard at work. When their opinions on any given subject did not mesh with his, they, too, were frightened of him.

Enlisting the help of a coach, the executive went to work to heighten his empathy through practice and feedback. His first step was to take a vacation to a foreign country where he did not speak the language. While there, he monitored his reactions to the unfamiliar and his openness to people who were different from him. When he returned home, humbled by his week abroad, the executive asked his coach to shadow him for parts of the day, several times a week, to critique how he treated people with new or different perspectives. At the same time, he consciously used on-the-job interactions as opportunities to practice "hearing" ideas that differed from his. Finally, the executive had himself videotaped in meetings and asked those who worked for and with him to critique his ability to acknowledge and understand the feelings of others. It took several months, but the executive's emotional intelligence did ultimately rise, and the improvement was reflected in his overall performance on the job.

It's important to emphasize that building one's emotional intelligence cannot—will not—happen without sincere desire and concerted effort. A brief seminar won't help; nor can one buy a how-to manual. It is much harder to learn to empathize—to internalize empathy as a natural response to people—than it is to become adept at regression analysis. But it can be done. "Nothing great was ever achieved without enthusiasm," wrote Ralph Waldo Emerson. If your goal is to become a real leader, these words can serve as a guidepost in your efforts to develop high emotional intelligence.

trivial demands take us away from the real work that needs to be done," she might explain. And she will go one step further and turn her anger into something constructive.

Self-awareness extends to a person's understanding of his or her values and goals. Someone who is highly self-aware knows where he is headed and why; so, for example, he will be able to be firm in turning down a job offer that is tempting financially but does not fit with his principles or long-term goals. A person who lacks self-awareness is apt to make decisions that bring on inner turmoil by treading on buried values. "The money looked good so I signed on," someone might say two years into a job, "but the work means so little to me that I'm constantly bored." The decisions of self-aware people mesh with their values; consequently, they often find work to be energizing.

How can one recognize self-awareness? First and foremost, it shows itself as candor and an ability to assess oneself realistically. People with high self-awareness are able to speak accurately and openly—although not necessarily effusively or confessionally—about their emotions and the impact they have on their work. For instance, one manager I know of was skeptical about a new personal-shopper service that her company, a major department-store chain, was about to introduce. Without prompting from her team or her boss, she offered them an explanation: "It's hard for me to get behind the rollout of this service," she admitted, "because I really wanted to run the project, but I wasn't selected. Bear with me while I deal with that." The manager did indeed examine her feelings; a week later, she was supporting the project fully.

Such self-knowledge often shows itself in the hiring process. Ask a candidate to describe a time he got carried away by his feelings and did something he later regretted. Self-aware candidates will be frank in admitting to failure—and will often tell their tales with a smile. One of the hallmarks of self-awareness is a self-deprecating sense of humor.

Self-awareness can also be identified during performance reviews. Self-aware people know—and are comfortable talking about—their limitations and strengths, and they often demonstrate a thirst for constructive criticism. By contrast, people with low self-awareness interpret the message that they need to improve as a threat or a sign of failure.

Self-aware people can also be recognized by their self-confidence. They have a firm grasp of their capabilities and are less likely to set themselves up to fail by, for example, overstretching on assignments. They know, too, when to ask for help. And the risks they take on the job are calculated. They won't ask for a challenge that they know they can't handle alone. They'll play to their strengths.

Consider the actions of a midlevel employee who was invited to sit in on a strategy meeting with her company's top executives. Although she was the most junior person in the room, she did not sit there quietly, listening in awestruck or fearful silence. She knew she had a head for clear logic and the skill to present ideas persuasively, and she offered cogent suggestions about the company's strategy. At the same time, her self-awareness stopped her from wandering into territory where she knew she was weak.

Despite the value of having self-aware people in the workplace, my research indicates that senior executives don't often give self-awareness the credit it deserves when they look for potential leaders. Many executives mistake candor about feelings for "wimpiness" and fail to give due respect to employees who openly acknowledge their shortcomings. Such people are too readily dismissed as "not tough enough" to lead others.

In fact, the opposite is true. In the first place, people generally admire and respect candor. Furthermore, leaders are constantly required to make judgment calls that require a candid assessment of capabilities—their own and those of others. Do we have the management expertise to acquire a competitor? Can we launch a new product within six months? People who assess themselves honestly—that is, self-aware people—are well suited to do the same for the organizations they run.

Self-Regulation

Biological impulses drive our emotions. We cannot do away with them—but we can do much to manage them. Self-regulation, which is like an ongoing inner conversation, is the component of emotional intelligence that frees us from being prisoners of our feelings. People engaged in such a conversation feel bad moods and emotional impulses just as everyone else does, but they find ways to control them and even to channel them in useful ways.

Imagine an executive who has just watched a team of his employees present a botched analysis to the company's board of directors. In the gloom that follows, the executive might find himself tempted to pound on the table in anger or kick over a chair. He could leap up and scream at the group. Or he might maintain a grim silence, glaring at everyone before stalking off.

But if he had a gift for self-regulation, he would choose a different approach. He would pick his words carefully, acknowledging the team's poor performance without rushing to any hasty judgment. He would then step back to consider the reasons for the failure. Are they personal—a lack of effort? Are there any mitigating factors? What was his role in the debacle? After considering these questions, he would call the team together, lay out the incident's consequences, and offer his feelings about it. He would then present his analysis of the problem and a well-considered solution.

Why does self-regulation matter so much for leaders? First of all, people who are in control of their feelings and impulses—that is, people who are reasonable—are able to create an environment of trust and fairness. In such an environment, politics and infighting are sharply reduced and productivity is high. Talented people flock to the organization and aren't tempted to leave. And self-regulation has a trickle-down effect. No one wants to be known as a hothead when the boss is known for her calm approach. Fewer bad moods at the top mean fewer throughout the organization.

Second, self-regulation is important for competitive reasons. Everyone knows that business today is rife with ambiguity and change. Companies merge and break apart regularly. Technology transforms work at a dizzying pace. People who have mastered their emotions are able to roll with the changes. When a new program is announced, they don't panic; instead, they are able to suspend judgment, seek out information, and listen to the executives as they explain the new program. As the initiative moves forward, these people are able to move with it.

Sometimes they even lead the way. Consider the case of a manager at a large manufacturing company. Like her colleagues, she had used a certain software program for five years. The program drove how she collected and reported data and how she thought about the company's strategy. One day, senior executives announced that a new program was to be installed that would radically change how information was gathered and assessed within the organization. While many people in the company complained bitterly about how disruptive the change would be, the manager mulled over the reasons for the new program and was convinced of its potential to improve performance. She eagerly attended training sessions—some of her colleagues refused to do so—and was eventually promoted to run several divisions, in part because she used the new technology so effectively.

I want to push the importance of self-regulation to leadership even further and make the case that it enhances integrity, which is not only a personal virtue but also an organizational strength. Many of the bad things that happen in companies are a function of impulsive behavior. People rarely plan to exaggerate profits, pad expense accounts, dip into the till, or abuse power for selfish ends. Instead, an opportunity presents itself, and people with low impulse control just say yes.

By contrast, consider the behavior of the senior executive at a large food company. The executive was scrupulously honest in his negotiations with local distributors. He would routinely lay out his cost structure in detail, thereby giving the distributors a realistic understanding of the company's pricing. This approach meant the executive couldn't always drive a hard bargain. Now, on occasion, he felt the urge to increase profits by withholding information about the company's costs. But he challenged that impulse—he saw that it made more sense in the long run to counteract it. His emotional self-regulation paid off in strong, lasting relationships with distributors that benefited the company more than any short-term financial gains would have.

The signs of emotional self-regulation, therefore, are easy to see: a propensity for reflection and thoughtfulness; comfort with ambiguity and change; and integrity—an ability to say no to impulsive urges.

Like self-awareness, self-regulation often does not get its due. People who can master their emotions are sometimes seen as cold fish—their considered responses are taken as a lack of passion. People with fiery temperaments are frequently thought of as "classic" leaders—their outbursts are considered hallmarks of charisma and power. But when such people make it to the top, their impulsiveness often works against them. In my research, extreme displays of negative emotion have never emerged as a driver of good leadership.

Motivation

If there is one trait that virtually all effective leaders have, it is motivation. They are driven to achieve beyond expectations—their own and everyone else's. The key word here is *achieve*. Plenty of people are motivated by external factors, such as a big salary or the status that comes from having an impressive title or being part of a prestigious company. By contrast, those with leadership potential are motivated by a deeply embedded desire to achieve for the sake of achievement.

If you are looking for leaders, how can you identify people who are motivated by the drive to achieve rather than by external rewards? The first sign is a passion for the work itself—such people seek out creative challenges, love to learn, and take great pride in a job well done. They also display an unflagging energy to do things better. People with such energy often seem restless with the status quo. They are persistent with their questions about why things are done one way rather than another; they are eager to explore new approaches to their work.

A cosmetics company manager, for example, was frustrated that he had to wait two weeks to get sales results from people in the field. He finally tracked down an automated phone system that would beep each of his salespeople at 5 pm every day. An automated message then prompted them to punch in their numbers—how many calls and sales they had made that day. The system shortened the feedback time on sales results from weeks to hours.

That story illustrates two other common traits of people who are driven to achieve. They are forever raising the performance bar, and they like to keep score. Take the performance bar first. During performance reviews, people with high levels of motivation might ask to be "stretched" by their superiors. Of course, an employee who combines self-awareness with internal motivation will recognize her limits—but she won't settle for objectives that seem too easy to fulfill.

And it follows naturally that people who are driven to do better also want a way of tracking progress—their own, their team's, and their company's. Whereas people with low achievement motivation are often fuzzy about results, those with high achievement motivation often keep score by tracking such hard measures as profitability or market share. I know of a money manager who starts and ends his day on the Internet, gauging the performance of his stock fund against four industry-set benchmarks.

Interestingly, people with high motivation remain optimistic even when the score is against them. In such cases, self-regulation combines with achievement motivation to overcome the frustration and depression that come after a setback or failure. Take the case of another portfolio manager at a large investment company. After several successful years, her fund tumbled for three consecutive quarters, leading three large institutional clients to shift their business elsewhere.

Some executives would have blamed the nosedive on circumstances outside their control; others might have seen the setback as evidence of personal failure. This portfolio manager, however, saw an opportunity to prove she could lead a turnaround. Two years later, when she was promoted to a very senior level in the company, she described the experience as "the best thing that ever happened to me; I learned so much from it."

Executives trying to recognize high levels of achievement motivation in their people can look for one last piece of evidence: commitment to the organization. When people love their jobs for the work itself, they often feel committed to the organizations that make that work possible. Committed employees are likely to stay with an organization even when they are pursued by headhunters waving money.

It's not difficult to understand how and why a motivation to achieve translates into strong leadership. If you set the performance bar high for yourself, you will do the same for the organization when you are in a position to do so. Likewise, a drive to surpass goals and an interest in keeping score can be contagious. Leaders with these traits can often build a team of managers around them with the same traits. And of course, optimism and organizational commitment are fundamental to leadership—just try to imagine running a company without them.

Empathy

Of all the dimensions of emotional intelligence, empathy is the most easily recognized. We have all felt the empathy of a sensitive teacher or friend; we have all been struck by its absence in an unfeeling coach or boss. But when it comes to business, we rarely hear people praised, let alone rewarded, for their empathy. The very word seems unbusinesslike, out of place amid the tough realities of the marketplace.

But empathy doesn't mean a kind of "I'm OK, you're OK" mushiness. For a leader, that is, it doesn't mean adopting other people's emotions as one's own and trying to please everybody. That would be a nightmare—it would make action impossible. Rather, empathy means thoughtfully considering employees' feelings—along with other factors—in the process of making intelligent decisions.

For an example of empathy in action, consider what happened when two giant brokerage companies merged, creating redundant jobs in all their divisions. One division manager called his people together and gave a gloomy speech that emphasized the number of people who would soon be fired. The manager of another division gave his people a different kind of speech. He was up-front about his own worry and confusion, and he promised to keep people informed and to treat everyone fairly.

The difference between these two managers was empathy. The first manager was too worried about his own fate to consider the feelings of his anxiety-stricken colleagues. The second knew intuitively what his people were feeling, and he acknowledged their fears with his words. Is it any surprise that the first manager saw his division sink as many demoralized people, especially the most talented, departed? By contrast, the second manager continued to be a strong leader, his best people stayed, and his division remained as productive as ever.

Empathy is particularly important today as a component of leadership for at least three reasons: the increasing use of teams; the rapid pace of globalization; and the growing need to retain talent.

Consider the challenge of leading a team. As anyone who has ever been a part of one can attest, teams are cauldrons of bubbling emotions. They are often charged with reaching a consensus—which is hard enough with two people and much more difficult as the numbers increase. Even in groups with as few as four or five members, alliances form and clashing agendas get set. A team's leader must be able to sense and understand the viewpoints of everyone around the table.

That's exactly what a marketing manager at a large information technology company was able to do when she was appointed to lead a troubled team. The group was in turmoil, overloaded by work and missing deadlines. Tensions were high among the members. Tinkering with procedures was not enough to bring the group together and make it an effective part of the company.

So the manager took several steps. In a series of one-on-one sessions, she took the time to listen to everyone in the group—what was frustrating them, how they rated their colleagues, whether they felt they had been ignored. And then she directed the team in a way that brought it together: She encouraged people to speak more openly about their frustrations, and she helped people raise constructive complaints during meetings. In short, her empathy allowed her to understand her team's emotional makeup. The result was not just heightened collaboration among members but also added business, as the team was called on for help by a wider range of internal clients.

Globalization is another reason for the rising importance of empathy for business leaders. Cross-cultural dialogue can easily lead to miscues and misunderstandings. Empathy is an antidote. People who have it are attuned to subtleties in body language; they can hear the message beneath the words being spoken. Beyond that, they have a deep understanding of both the existence and the importance of cultural and ethnic differences.

Consider the case of an American consultant whose team had just pitched a project to a potential Japanese client. In its dealings with Americans, the team was accustomed to being bombarded with questions after such a proposal, but this time it was greeted with a long silence. Other members of the team, taking the silence as disapproval, were ready to pack and leave. The lead consultant gestured them to stop. Although he was not particularly familiar with Japanese culture, he read the client's face and posture and sensed not rejection but interest—even deep consideration. He was right: When the client finally spoke, it was to give the consulting firm the job.

Finally, empathy plays a key role in the retention of talent, particularly in today's information economy. Leaders have always needed empathy to develop and keep good people, but today the stakes are higher. When good people leave, they take the company's knowledge with them.

That's where coaching and mentoring come in. It has repeatedly been shown that coaching and mentoring pay off not just in better performance but also in increased job satisfaction and decreased turnover. But what makes coaching and mentoring work best is the nature of the relationship. Outstanding coaches and mentors get inside the heads of the people they are helping. They sense how to give effective feedback. They know when to push for better performance and when to hold back. In the way they motivate their protégés, they demonstrate empathy in action.

In what is probably sounding like a refrain, let me repeat that empathy doesn't get much respect in business. People wonder how leaders can make hard decisions if they are "feeling" for all the people who will be affected. But leaders with empathy do more than sympathize with people around them: They use their knowledge to improve their companies in subtle but important ways.

Social Skill

The first three components of emotional intelligence are self-management skills. The last two, empathy and social skill, concern a person's ability to manage relationships with others. As a component of emotional intelligence, social skill is not as simple as it sounds. It's not just a matter of friendliness, although people with high levels of social skill are rarely mean-spirited. Social skill, rather, is friendliness with a purpose: moving people in the direction you desire, whether that's agreement on a new marketing strategy or enthusiasm about a new product.

Socially skilled people tend to have a wide circle of acquaintances, and they have a knack for finding common ground with people of all kinds—a knack for building rapport. That doesn't mean they socialize continually; it means they work according to the assumption that nothing important gets done alone. Such people have a network in place when the time for action comes.

Social skill is the culmination of the other dimensions of emotional intelligence. People tend to be very effective at managing relationships when they can understand and control their own emotions and can empathize with the feelings of others. Even motivation contributes to social skill. Remember that people who are driven to achieve tend to be optimistic, even in the face of setbacks or failure. When people are upbeat, their "glow" is cast upon conversations and other social encounters. They are popular, and for good reason.

Because it is the outcome of the other dimensions of emotional intelligence, social skill is recognizable on the job in many ways that will by now sound familiar. Socially skilled people, for instance, are adept at managing teams—that's their empathy at work. Likewise, they are expert persuaders—a manifestation of self-awareness, self-regulation, and empathy combined. Given those skills, good persuaders know when to make an emotional plea, for instance, and when an appeal to reason will work better. And motivation, when publicly visible, makes such people excellent collaborators; their passion for the work spreads to others, and they are driven to find solutions.

But sometimes social skill shows itself in ways the other emotional intelligence components do not. For instance, socially skilled people may at times appear not to be working while at work. They seem to be idly schmoozing—chatting in the hallways with colleagues or joking around with people who are not even connected to their "real" jobs. Socially skilled people, however, don't think it makes sense to arbitrarily limit the scope of their relationships. They build bonds widely because they know that in these fluid times, they may need help someday from people they are just getting to know today.

For example, consider the case of an executive in the strategy department of a global computer manufacturer. By 1993, he was convinced that the company's future lay with the Internet. Over the course of the next year, he found kindred spirits and used his social skill to stitch together a virtual community that cut across levels, divisions, and nations. He then used this de facto team to put up a corporate Web site, among the first by a major company. And, on his own initiative, with no budget or formal status, he signed up the company to participate in an annual Internet industry convention. Calling on his allies and persuading various divisions to donate funds, he recruited more than 50 people from a dozen different units to represent the company at the convention.

Management took notice: Within a year of the conference, the executive's team formed the basis for the company's first Internet division, and he was formally put in charge of it. To get there, the executive had ignored conventional boundaries, forging and maintaining connections with people in every corner of the organization.

Is social skill considered a key leadership capability in most companies? The answer is yes, especially when compared with the other components of emotional intelligence. People seem to know intuitively that leaders need to manage relationships effectively; no leader is an island. After all, the leader's task is to get work done through other people, and social skill makes that possible. A leader who cannot express her empathy may as well not have it at all. And a leader's motivation will be useless if he cannot communicate his passion to the organization. Social skill allows leaders to put their emotional intelligence to work.

It would be foolish to assert that good-old-fashioned IQ and technical ability are not important ingredients in strong leadership. But the recipe would not be complete without emotional intelligence. It was once thought that the components of emotional intelligence were "nice to have" in business leaders. But now we know that, for the sake of performance, these are ingredients that leaders "need to have."

It is fortunate, then, that emotional intelligence can be learned. The process is not easy. It takes time and, most of all, commitment. But the benefits that come from having a well-developed emotional intelligence, both for the individual and for the organization, make it worth the effort.

Originally published in June 1996. Reprint R0401H

What Makes an Effective Executive

by Peter F. Drucker

AN EFFECTIVE EXECUTIVE DOES NOT need to be a leader in the sense that the term is now most commonly used. Harry Truman did not have one ounce of charisma, for example, yet he was among the most effective chief executives in U.S. history. Similarly, some of the best business and nonprofit CEOs I've worked with over a 65-year consulting career were not stereotypical leaders. They were all over the map in terms of their personalities, attitudes, values, strengths, and weaknesses. They ranged from extroverted to nearly reclusive, from easygoing to controlling, from generous to parsimonious.

What made them all effective is that they followed the same eight practices:

- They asked, "What needs to be done?"

- They asked, "What is right for the enterprise?"

- They developed action plans.

- They took responsibility for decisions.

- They took responsibility for communicating.

- They were focused on opportunities rather than problems.

- They ran productive meetings.

- They thought and said "we" rather than "I."

The first two practices gave them the knowledge they needed. The next four helped them convert this knowledge into effective action. The last two ensured that the whole organization felt responsible and accountable.

Get the Knowledge You Need

The first practice is to ask what needs to be done. Note that the question is not "What do I want to do?" Asking what has to be done, and taking the question seriously, is crucial for managerial success. Failure to ask this question will render even the ablest executive ineffectual.

When Truman became president in 1945, he knew exactly what he wanted to do: complete the economic and social reforms of Roosevelt's New Deal, which had been deferred by World War II. As soon as he asked what needed to be done, though, Truman realized that foreign affairs had absolute priority. He organized his working day so that it began with tutorials on foreign policy by the secretaries of state and defense. As a result, he became the most effective president in foreign affairs the United States has ever known. He contained Communism in both Europe and Asia and, with the Marshall Plan, triggered 50 years of worldwide economic growth.

Similarly, Jack Welch realized that what needed to be done at General Electric when he took over as chief executive was not the overseas expansion he wanted to launch. It was getting rid of GE businesses that, no matter how profitable, could not be number one or number two in their industries.

The answer to the question "What needs to be done?" almost always contains more than one urgent task. But effective executives do not splinter themselves. They concentrate on one task if at all possible. If they are among those people—a sizable minority—who work best with a change of pace in their working day, they pick two tasks. I have never encountered an executive who remains effective while tackling more than two tasks at a time. Hence, after asking what

Idea in Brief

Worried that you're not a born leader? That you lack charisma, the right talents, or some other secret ingredient? No need: leadership isn't about personality or talent. In fact, the best leaders exhibit wildly different personalities, attitudes, values, and strengths—they're extroverted or reclusive, easygoing or controlling, generous or parsimonious, numbers or vision oriented.

So what do effective leaders have in common? They get the right things done, in the right ways—by following eight simple rules:

- Ask what needs to be done.

- Ask what's right for the enterprise.

- Develop action plans.

- Take responsibility for decisions.

- Take responsibility for communicating.

- Focus on opportunities, not problems.

- Run productive meetings.

- Think and say "We," not "I."

Using discipline to apply these rules, you gain the knowledge you need to make smart decisions, convert that knowledge into effective action, and ensure accountability throughout your organization.

needs to be done, the effective executive sets priorities and sticks to them. For a CEO, the priority task might be redefining the company's mission. For a unit head, it might be redefining the unit's relationship with headquarters. Other tasks, no matter how important or appealing, are postponed. However, after completing the original top-priority task, the executive resets priorities rather than moving on to number two from the original list. He asks, "What must be done now?" This generally results in new and different priorities.

To refer again to America's best-known CEO: Every five years, according to his autobiography, Jack Welch asked himself, "What needs to be done *now?*" And every time, he came up with a new and different priority.

But Welch also thought through another issue before deciding where to concentrate his efforts for the next five years. He asked himself which of the two or three tasks at the top of the list he himself was best suited to undertake. Then he concentrated on that

Idea in Practice

Get the Knowledge You Need

Ask what needs to be done. When Jack Welch asked this question while taking over as CEO at General Electric, he realized that dropping GE businesses that couldn't be first or second in their industries was essential—not the overseas expansion he had wanted to launch. Once you know what must be done, identify tasks you're best at, concentrating on one at a time. After completing a task, reset priorities based on new realities.

Ask what's right for the enterprise. Don't agonize over what's best for owners, investors, employees, or customers. Decisions that are right for your *enterprise* are ultimately right for all stakeholders.

Convert Your Knowledge into Action

Develop action plans. Devise plans that specify *desired results* and *constraints* (Is the course of action legal and compatible with the company's mission, values, and policies?). Include *check-in points* and *implications for how you'll spend your time*. And *revise* plans to reflect new opportunities.

Take responsibility for decisions. Ensure that each decision specifies who's accountable for carrying it out, when it must be implemented, who'll be affected by it, and who must be informed. Regularly review decisions, especially hires and promotions. This enables you to correct poor decisions before doing real damage.

Take responsibility for communicating. Get input from superiors, subordinates, and peers on your action plans. Let each know what information you need to get the

task; the others he delegated. Effective executives try to focus on jobs they'll do especially well. They know that enterprises perform if top management performs—and don't if it doesn't.

Effective executives' second practice—fully as important as the first—is to ask, "Is this the right thing for the enterprise?" They do not ask if it's right for the owners, the stock price, the employees, or the executives. Of course they know that shareholders, employees, and executives are important constituencies who have to support a decision, or at least acquiesce in it, if the choice is to be effective. They know that the share price is important not only for the shareholders but also for the enterprise, since the price/earnings ratio sets the cost job done. Pay equal attention to peers' and superiors' information needs.

Focus on opportunities, not problems. You get results by exploiting opportunities, not solving problems. Identify changes inside and outside your organization (new technologies, product innovations, new market structures), asking "How can we exploit this change to benefit our enterprise?" Then match your best people with the best opportunities.

Ensure Companywide Accountability
Run productive meetings. Articulate each meeting's purpose (Making an announcement? Delivering a report?). Terminate the meeting once the purpose is accomplished. Follow up with short communications summarizing the discussion, spelling out new work assignments and deadlines for completing them. General Motors CEO Alfred Sloan's legendary mastery of meeting follow-up helped secure GM's industry dominance in the mid-twentieth century.

Think and say "We," not "I." Your authority comes from your organization's trust in you. To get the best results, always consider your organization's needs and opportunities before your own.

of capital. But they also know that a decision that isn't right for the enterprise will ultimately not be right for any of the stakeholders.

This second practice is especially important for executives at family owned or family run businesses—the majority of businesses in every country—particularly when they're making decisions about people. In the successful family company, a relative is promoted only if he or she is measurably superior to all nonrelatives on the same level. At DuPont, for instance, all top managers (except the controller and lawyer) were family members in the early years when the firm was run as a family business. All male descendants of the founders were entitled to entry-level jobs at the company. Beyond the entrance level, a family member got a promotion only if a panel composed primarily of nonfamily managers judged the person to be superior in ability and performance to all other employees at the same level. The same rule was observed for a century in the highly successful British family business J. Lyons & Company (now part of a major conglomerate) when it dominated the British food-service and hotel industries.

Asking "What is right for the enterprise?" does not guarantee that the right decision will be made. Even the most brilliant executive is human and thus prone to mistakes and prejudices. But failure to ask the question virtually guarantees the *wrong* decision.

Write an Action Plan

Executives are doers; they execute. Knowledge is useless to executives until it has been translated into deeds. But before springing into action, the executive needs to plan his course. He needs to think about desired results, probable restraints, future revisions, check-in points, and implications for how he'll spend his time.

First, the executive defines desired results by asking: "What contributions should the enterprise expect from me over the next 18 months to two years? What results will I commit to? With what deadlines?" Then he considers the restraints on action: "Is this course of action ethical? Is it acceptable within the organization? Is it legal? Is it compatible with the mission, values, and policies of the organization?" Affirmative answers don't guarantee that the action will be effective. But violating these restraints is certain to make it both wrong and ineffectual.

The action plan is a statement of intentions rather than a commitment. It must not become a straitjacket. It should be revised often, because every success creates new opportunities. So does every failure. The same is true for changes in the business environment, in the market, and especially in people within the enterprise—all these changes demand that the plan be revised. A written plan should anticipate the need for flexibility.

In addition, the action plan needs to create a system for checking the results against the expectations. Effective executives usually build two such checks into their action plans. The first check comes halfway through the plan's time period; for example, at nine months. The second occurs at the end, before the next action plan is drawn up.

Finally, the action plan has to become the basis for the executive's time management. Time is an executive's scarcest and most precious resource. And organizations—whether government agencies, businesses, or nonprofits—are inherently time wasters. The action plan will prove useless unless it's allowed to determine how the executive spends his or her time.

Napoleon allegedly said that no successful battle ever followed its plan. Yet Napoleon also planned every one of his battles, far more meticulously than any earlier general had done. Without an action plan, the executive becomes a prisoner of events. And without check-ins to reexamine the plan as events unfold, the executive has no way of knowing which events really matter and which are only noise.

Act

When they translate plans into action, executives need to pay particular attention to decision making, communication, opportunities (as opposed to problems), and meetings. I'll consider these one at a time.

Take responsibility for decisions

A decision has not been made until people know:

- the name of the person accountable for carrying it out;

- the deadline;

- the names of the people who will be affected by the decision and therefore have to know about, understand, and approve it—or at least not be strongly opposed to it—and

- the names of the people who have to be informed of the decision, even if they are not directly affected by it.

An extraordinary number of organizational decisions run into trouble because these bases aren't covered. One of my clients,

30 years ago, lost its leadership position in the fast-growing Japanese market because the company, after deciding to enter into a joint venture with a new Japanese partner, never made clear who was to inform the purchasing agents that the partner defined its specifications in meters and kilograms rather than feet and pounds—and nobody ever did relay that information.

It's just as important to review decisions periodically—at a time that's been agreed on in advance—as it is to make them carefully in the first place. That way, a poor decision can be corrected before it does real damage. These reviews can cover anything from the results to the assumptions underlying the decision.

Such a review is especially important for the most crucial and most difficult of all decisions, the ones about hiring or promoting people. Studies of decisions about people show that only one-third of such choices turn out to be truly successful. One-third are likely to be draws—neither successes nor outright failures. And one-third are failures, pure and simple. Effective executives know this and check up (six to nine months later) on the results of their people decisions. If they find that a decision has not had the desired results, they don't conclude that the person has not performed. They conclude, instead, that they themselves made a mistake. In a well-managed enterprise, it is understood that people who fail in a new job, especially after a promotion, may not be the ones to blame.

Executives also owe it to the organization and to their fellow workers not to tolerate nonperforming individuals in important jobs. It may not be the employees' fault that they are underperforming, but even so, they have to be removed. People who have failed in a new job should be given the choice to go back to a job at their former level and salary. This option is rarely exercised; such people, as a rule, leave voluntarily, at least when their employers are U.S. firms. But the very existence of the option can have a powerful effect, encouraging people to leave safe, comfortable jobs and take risky new assignments. The organization's performance depends on employees' willingness to take such chances.

A systematic decision review can be a powerful tool for self-development, too. Checking the results of a decision against its expectations shows executives what their strengths are, where they need to improve, and where they lack knowledge or information. It shows them their biases. Very often it shows them that their decisions didn't produce results because they didn't put the right people on the job. Allocating the best people to the right positions is a crucial, tough job that many executives slight, in part because the best people are already too busy. Systematic decision review also shows executives their own weaknesses, particularly the areas in which they are simply incompetent. In these areas, smart executives don't make decisions or take actions. They delegate. Everyone has such areas; there's no such thing as a universal executive genius.

Most discussions of decision making assume that only senior executives make decisions or that only senior executives' decisions matter. This is a dangerous mistake. Decisions are made at every level of the organization, beginning with individual professional contributors and frontline supervisors. These apparently low-level decisions are extremely important in a knowledge-based organization. Knowledge workers are supposed to know more about their areas of specialization—for example, tax accounting—than anybody else, so their decisions are likely to have an impact throughout the company. Making good decisions is a crucial skill at every level. It needs to be taught explicitly to everyone in organizations that are based on knowledge.

Take responsibility for communicating
Effective executives make sure that both their action plans and their information needs are understood. Specifically, this means that they share their plans with and ask for comments from all their colleagues—superiors, subordinates, and peers. At the same time, they let each person know what information they'll need to get the job done. The information flow from subordinate to boss is usually what gets the most attention. But executives need to pay equal attention to peers' and superiors' information needs.

We all know, thanks to Chester Barnard's 1938 classic *The Functions of the Executive,* that organizations are held together by information rather than by ownership or command. Still, far too many executives behave as if information and its flow were the job of the information specialist—for example, the accountant. As a result, they get an enormous amount of data they do not need and cannot use, but little of the information they do need. The best way around this problem is for each executive to identify the information he needs, ask for it, and keep pushing until he gets it.

Focus on opportunities

Good executives focus on opportunities rather than problems. Problems have to be taken care of, of course; they must not be swept under the rug. But problem solving, however necessary, does not produce results. It prevents damage. Exploiting opportunities produces results.

Above all, effective executives treat change as an opportunity rather than a threat. They systematically look at changes, inside and outside the corporation, and ask, "How can we exploit this change as an opportunity for our enterprise?" Specifically, executives scan these seven situations for opportunities:

- an unexpected success or failure in their own enterprise, in a competing enterprise, or in the industry;

- a gap between what is and what could be in a market, process, product, or service (for example, in the nineteenth century, the paper industry concentrated on the 10% of each tree that became wood pulp and totally neglected the possibilities in the remaining 90%, which became waste);

- innovation in a process, product, or service, whether inside or outside the enterprise or its industry;

- changes in industry structure and market structure;

- demographics;

- changes in mind-set, values, perception, mood, or meaning; and

- new knowledge or a new technology.

Effective executives also make sure that problems do not overwhelm opportunities. In most companies, the first page of the monthly management report lists key problems. It's far wiser to list opportunities on the first page and leave problems for the second page. Unless there is a true catastrophe, problems are not discussed in management meetings until opportunities have been analyzed and properly dealt with.

Staffing is another important aspect of being opportunity focused. Effective executives put their best people on opportunities rather than on problems. One way to staff for opportunities is to ask each member of the management group to prepare two lists every six months—a list of opportunities for the entire enterprise and a list of the best-performing people throughout the enterprise. These are discussed, then melded into two master lists, and the best people are matched with the best opportunities. In Japan, by the way, this matchup is considered a major HR task in a big corporation or government department; that practice is one of the key strengths of Japanese business.

Make meetings productive

The most visible, powerful, and, arguably, effective nongovernmental executive in the America of World War II and the years thereafter was not a businessman. It was Francis Cardinal Spellman, the head of the Roman Catholic Archdiocese of New York and adviser to several U.S. presidents. When Spellman took over, the diocese was bankrupt and totally demoralized. His successor inherited the leadership position in the American Catholic church. Spellman often said that during his waking hours he was alone only twice each day, for 25 minutes each time: when he said Mass in his private chapel after getting up in the morning and when he said his evening prayers before going to bed. Otherwise he was always with people in a meeting, starting at breakfast with one Catholic organization and ending at dinner with another.

Top executives aren't quite as imprisoned as the archbishop of a major Catholic diocese. But every study of the executive workday has found that even junior executives and professionals are with other people—that is, in a meeting of some sort—more than half of every business day. The only exceptions are a few senior researchers. Even a conversation with only one other person is a meeting. Hence, if they are to be effective, executives must make meetings productive. They must make sure that meetings are work sessions rather than bull sessions.

The key to running an effective meeting is to decide in advance what kind of meeting it will be. Different kinds of meetings require different forms of preparation and different results.

A meeting to prepare a statement, an announcement, or a press release. For this to be productive, one member has to prepare a draft beforehand. At the meeting's end, a preappointed member has to take responsibility for disseminating the final text.

A meeting to make an announcement—for example, an organizational change. This meeting should be confined to the announcement and a discussion about it.

A meeting in which one member reports. Nothing but the report should be discussed.

A meeting in which several or all members report. Either there should be no discussion at all or the discussion should be limited to questions for clarification. Alternatively, for each report there could be a short discussion in which all participants may ask questions. If this is the format, the reports should be distributed to all participants well before the meeting. At this kind of meeting, each report should be limited to a preset time—for example, 15 minutes.

A meeting to inform the convening executive. The executive should listen and ask questions. He or she should sum up but not make a presentation.

A meeting whose only function is to allow the participants to be in the executive's presence. Cardinal Spellman's breakfast and dinner meetings were of that kind. There is no way to make these meetings productive. They are the penalties of rank. Senior executives are effective to the extent to which they can prevent such meetings from encroaching on their workdays. Spellman, for instance, was effective in large part because he confined such meetings to breakfast and dinner and kept the rest of his working day free of them.

Making a meeting productive takes a good deal of self-discipline. It requires that executives determine what kind of meeting is appropriate and then stick to that format. It's also necessary to terminate the meeting as soon as its specific purpose has been accomplished. Good executives don't raise another matter for discussion. They sum up and adjourn.

Good follow-up is just as important as the meeting itself. The great master of follow-up was Alfred Sloan, the most effective business executive I have ever known. Sloan, who headed General Motors from the 1920s until the 1950s, spent most of his six working days a week in meetings—three days a week in formal committee meetings with a set membership, the other three days in ad hoc meetings with individual GM executives or with a small group of executives. At the beginning of a formal meeting, Sloan announced the meeting's purpose. He then listened. He never took notes and he rarely spoke except to clarify a confusing point. At the end he summed up, thanked the participants, and left. Then he immediately wrote a short memo addressed to one attendee of the meeting. In that note, he summarized the discussion and its conclusions and spelled out any work assignment decided upon in the meeting (including a decision to hold another meeting on the subject or to study an issue). He specified the deadline and the executive who was to be accountable for the assignment. He sent a copy of the memo to everyone who'd been present at the meeting. It was through these memos—each a small masterpiece—that Sloan made himself into an outstandingly effective executive.

Effective executives know that any given meeting is either productive or a total waste of time.

Think and Say "We"

The final practice is this: Don't think or say "I." Think and say "we." Effective executives know that they have ultimate responsibility, which can be neither shared nor delegated. But they have authority only because they have the trust of the organization. This means that they think of the needs and the opportunities of the organization before they think of their own needs and opportunities. This one may sound simple; it isn't, but it needs to be strictly observed.

We've just reviewed eight practices of effective executives. I'm going to throw in one final, bonus practice. This one's so important that I'll elevate it to the level of a rule: *Listen first, speak last.*

Effective executives differ widely in their personalities, strengths, weaknesses, values, and beliefs. All they have in common is that they get the right things done. Some are born effective. But the demand is much too great to be satisfied by extraordinary talent. Effectiveness is a discipline. And, like every discipline, effectiveness *can* be learned and *must* be earned.

Originally published in June 2004. Reprint R0406C

What Leaders Really Do

by John P. Kotter

LEADERSHIP IS DIFFERENT FROM MANAGEMENT, but not for the reasons most people think. Leadership isn't mystical and mysterious. It has nothing to do with having "charisma" or other exotic personality traits. It is not the province of a chosen few. Nor is leadership necessarily better than management or a replacement for it.

Rather, leadership and management are two distinctive and complementary systems of action. Each has its own function and characteristic activities. Both are necessary for success in an increasingly complex and volatile business environment.

Most U.S. corporations today are over-managed and underled. They need to develop their capacity to exercise leadership. Successful corporations don't wait for leaders to come along. They actively seek out people with leadership potential and expose them to career experiences designed to develop that potential. Indeed, with careful selection, nurturing, and encouragement, dozens of people can play important leadership roles in a business organization.

But while improving their ability to lead, companies should remember that strong leadership with weak management is no better, and is sometimes actually worse, than the reverse. The real challenge is to combine strong leadership and strong management and use each to balance the other.

Of course, not everyone can be good at both leading and managing. Some people have the capacity to become excellent managers but not strong leaders. Others have great leadership potential but, for a variety of reasons, have great difficulty becoming strong managers. Smart companies value both kinds of people and work hard to make them a part of the team.

But when it comes to preparing people for executive jobs, such companies rightly ignore the recent literature that says people cannot manage *and* lead. They try to develop leader-managers. Once companies understand the fundamental difference between leadership and management, they can begin to groom their top people to provide both.

The Difference Between Management and Leadership

Management is about coping with complexity. Its practices and procedures are largely a response to one of the most significant developments of the twentieth century: the emergence of large organizations. Without good management, complex enterprises tend to become chaotic in ways that threaten their very existence. Good management brings a degree of order and consistency to key dimensions like the quality and profitability of products.

Leadership, by contrast, is about coping with change. Part of the reason it has become so important in recent years is that the business world has become more competitive and more volatile. Faster technological change, greater international competition, the deregulation of markets, overcapacity in capital-intensive industries, an unstable oil cartel, raiders with junk bonds, and the changing demographics of the work-force are among the many factors that have contributed to this shift. The net result is that doing what was done yesterday, or doing it 5% better, is no longer a formula for success. Major changes are more and more necessary to survive and compete effectively in this new environment. More change always demands more leadership.

Consider a simple military analogy: A peacetime army can usually survive with good administration and management up and down

Idea in Brief

The most pernicious half-truth about leadership is that it's just a matter of charisma and vision—you either have it or you don't. The fact of the matter is that leadership skills are not innate. They can be acquired, and honed. But first you have to appreciate how they differ from management skills.

Management is about coping with *complexity*; it brings order and predictability to a situation. But that's no longer enough—to succeed, companies must be able to adapt to change. Leadership,

then, is about learning how to cope with rapid *change*.

How does this distinction play out?

- Management involves planning and budgeting. Leadership involves setting direction.

- Management involves organizing and staffing. Leadership involves aligning people.

- Management provides control and solves problems. Leadership provides motivation.

the hierarchy, coupled with good leadership concentrated at the very top. A wartime army, however, needs competent leadership at all levels. No one yet has figured out how to manage people effectively into battle; they must be led.

These two different functions—coping with complexity and coping with change—shape the characteristic activities of management and leadership. Each system of action involves deciding what needs to be done, creating networks of people and relationships that can accomplish an agenda, and then trying to ensure that those people actually do the job. But each accomplishes these three tasks in different ways.

Companies manage complexity first by *planning and budgeting*—setting targets or goals for the future (typically for the next month or year), establishing detailed steps for achieving those targets, and then allocating resources to accomplish those plans. By contrast, leading an organization to constructive change begins by *setting a direction*—developing a vision of the future (often the distant future) along with strategies for producing the changes needed to achieve that vision.

Management develops the capacity to achieve its plan by *organizing and staffing*—creating an organizational structure and set of jobs for accomplishing plan requirements, staffing the jobs

Idea in Practice

Management and leadership both involve deciding what needs to be done, creating networks of people to accomplish the agenda, and ensuring that the work actually gets done. Their work is complementary, but each system of action goes about the tasks in different ways.

1. Planning and budgeting versus setting direction. The aim of management is predictability—orderly results. Leadership's function is to produce change. Setting the direction of that change, therefore, is essential work. There's nothing mystical about this work, but it is more inductive than planning and budgeting. It involves the search for patterns and relationships. And it doesn't produce detailed plans; instead, direction-setting results in visions and the overarching strategies for realizing them.

> *Example:* In mature industries, increased competition usually dampens growth. But at American Express, Lou Gerstner bucked this trend, successfully crafting a vision of a dynamic enterprise.
>
> The new direction he set wasn't a mere attention-grabbing scheme—it was the result of asking fundamental questions about market and competitive forces.

2. Organizing and staffing versus aligning people. Managers look for the right fit between people and jobs. This is essentially a design problem: setting up systems to ensure that plans are implemented precisely and efficiently. Leaders, however, look for the right fit between people and the vision. This is more of a communication problem. It involves getting a large number of people, inside and outside the company, first to believe in an alternative future—and then to take initiative based on that shared vision.

3. Controlling activities and solving problems versus motivating and inspiring. Management strives to make it easy for people to complete routine jobs day after day. But since high energy is essential to overcoming the barriers to change, leaders attempt to touch people at their deepest levels—by stirring in them a sense of belonging, idealism, and self-esteem.

> *Example:* At Procter & Gamble's paper products division, Richard Nicolosi underscored the message that "each of us is a leader" by pushing responsibility down to newly formed teams. An entrepreneurial attitude took root, and profits rebounded.

with qualified individuals, communicating the plan to those people, delegating responsibility for carrying out the plan, and devising systems to monitor implementation. The equivalent leadership activity, however, is *aligning people*. This means communicating the new direction to those who can create coalitions that understand the vision and are committed to its achievement.

Finally, management ensures plan accomplishment by *controlling and problem solving*—monitoring results versus the plan in some detail, both formally and informally, by means of reports, meetings, and other tools; identifying deviations; and then planning and organizing to solve the problems. But for leadership, achieving a vision requires *motivating and inspiring*—keeping people moving in the right direction, despite major obstacles to change, by appealing to basic but often untapped human needs, values, and emotions.

A closer examination of each of these activities will help clarify the skills leaders need.

Setting a Direction Versus Planning and Budgeting

Since the function of leadership is to produce change, setting the direction of that change is fundamental to leadership. Setting direction is never the same as planning or even long-term planning, although people often confuse the two. Planning is a management process, deductive in nature and designed to produce orderly results, not change. Setting a direction is more inductive. Leaders gather a broad range of data and look for patterns, relationships, and linkages that help explain things. What's more, the direction-setting aspect of leadership does not produce plans; it creates vision and strategies. These describe a business, technology, or corporate culture in terms of what it should become over the long term and articulate a feasible way of achieving this goal.

Most discussions of vision have a tendency to degenerate into the mystical. The implication is that a vision is something mysterious that mere mortals, even talented ones, could never hope to have. But developing good business direction isn't magic. It is a tough, sometimes exhausting process of gathering and analyzing information.

Aligning People: Chuck Trowbridge and Bob Crandall at Eastman Kodak

EASTMAN KODAK ENTERED THE copy business in the early 1970s, concentrating on technically sophisticated machines that sold, on average, for about $60,000 each. Over the next decade, this business grew to nearly $1 billion in revenues. But costs were high, profits were hard to find, and problems were nearly everywhere. In 1984, Kodak had to write off $40 million in inventory. Most people at the company knew there were problems, but they couldn't agree on how to solve them. So in his first two months as general manager of the new copy products group, established in 1984, Chuck Trowbridge met with nearly every key person inside his group, as well as with people elsewhere at Kodak who could be important to the copier business. An especially crucial area was the engineering and manufacturing organization, headed by Bob Crandall.

Trowbridge and Crandall's vision for engineering and manufacturing was simple: to become a world-class manufacturing operation and to create a less bureaucratic and more decentralized organization. Still, this message was difficult to convey because it was such a radical departure from previous communications, not only in the copy products group but throughout most of Kodak. So Crandall set up dozens of vehicles to emphasize the new direction and align people to it: weekly meetings with his own 12 direct reports; monthly "copy product forums" in which a different employee from each of his departments would meet with him as a group; discussions of recent improvements and new projects to achieve still better results; and quarterly "State of the Department" meetings, where his managers met with everybody in their own departments.

Once a month, Crandall and all those who reported to him would also meet with 80 to 100 people from some area of his organization to discuss anything they wanted. To align his biggest supplier—the Kodak Apparatus Division,

People who articulate such visions aren't magicians but broad-based strategic thinkers who are willing to take risks.

Nor do visions and strategies have to be brilliantly innovative; in fact, some of the best are not. Effective business visions regularly have an almost mundane quality, usually consisting of ideas that are already well known. The particular combination or patterning of the ideas may be new, but sometimes even that is not the case.

which supplied one-third of the parts used in design and manufacturing—he and his managers met with the top management of that group over lunch every Thursday. Later, he created a format called "business meetings," where his managers meet with 12 to 20 people on a specific topic, such as inventory or master scheduling. The goal: to get all of his 1,500 employees in at least one of these focused business meetings each year.

Trowbridge and Crandall also enlisted written communication in their cause. A four- to eight-page "Copy Products Journal" was sent to employees once a month. A program called "Dialog Letters" gave employees the opportunity to anonymously ask questions of Crandall and his top managers and be guaranteed a reply. But the most visible and powerful written communications were the charts. In a main hallway near the cafeteria, these huge charts vividly reported the quality, cost, and delivery results for each product, measured against difficult targets. A hundred smaller versions of these charts were scattered throughout the manufacturing area, reporting quality levels and costs for specific work groups.

Results of this intensive alignment process began to appear within six months, and still more surfaced after a year. These successes made the message more credible and helped get more people on board. Between 1984 and 1988, quality on one of the main product lines increased nearly 100-fold. Defects per unit went from 30 to 0.3. Over a three-year period, costs on another product line went down nearly 24%. Deliveries on schedule increased from 82% in 1985 to 95% in 1987. Inventory levels dropped by over 50% between 1984 and 1988, even though the volume of products was increasing. And productivity, measured in units per manufacturing employee, more than doubled between 1985 and 1988.

For example, when CEO Jan Carlzon articulated his vision to make Scandinavian Airlines System (SAS) the best airline in the world for the frequent business traveler, he was not saying anything that everyone in the airline industry didn't already know. Business travelers fly more consistently than other market segments and are generally willing to pay higher fares. Thus, focusing on business customers offers an airline the possibility of high margins, steady business, and

Setting a Direction: Lou Gerstner at American Express

WHEN LOU GERSTNER BECAME PRESIDENT of the Travel Related Services (TRS) arm at American Express in 1979, the unit was facing one of its biggest challenges in AmEx's 130-year history. Hundreds of banks offering or planning to introduce credit cards through Visa and MasterCard that would compete with the American Express card. And more than two dozen financial service firms were coming into the traveler's checks business. In a mature marketplace, this increase in competition usually reduces margins and prohibits growth.

But that was not how Gerstner saw the business. Before joining American Express, he had spent five years as a consultant to TRS, analyzing the money-losing travel division and the increasingly competitive card operation. Gerstner and his team asked fundamental questions about the economics, market, and competition and developed a deep understanding of the business. In the process, he began to craft a vision of TRS that looked nothing like a 130-year-old company in a mature industry.

Gerstner thought TRS had the potential to become a dynamic and growing enterprise, despite the onslaught of Visa and MasterCard competition from thousands of banks. The key was to focus on the global marketplace and, specifically, on the relatively affluent customer American Express had been traditionally serving with top-of-the-line products. By further segmenting this market, aggressively developing a broad range of new products and services, and investing to increase productivity and to lower costs, TRS could provide the best service possible to customers who had enough discretionary income to buy many more services from TRS than they had in the past.

Within a week of his appointment, Gerstner brought together the people running the card organization and questioned all the principles by which they conducted their business. In particular, he challenged two widely shared beliefs—that the division should have only one product, the green card, and that this product was limited in potential for growth and innovation.

---

considerable growth. But in an industry known more for bureaucracy than vision, no company had ever put these simple ideas together and dedicated itself to implementing them. SAS did, and it worked.

What's crucial about a vision is not its originality but how well it serves the interests of important constituencies—customers,

Gerstner also moved quickly to develop a more entrepreneurial culture, to hire and train people who would thrive in it, and to clearly communicate to them the overall direction. He and other top managers rewarded intelligent risk taking. To make entrepreneurship easier, they discouraged unnecessary bureaucracy. They also upgraded hiring standards and created the TRS Graduate Management Program, which offered high-potential young people special training, an enriched set of experiences, and an unusual degree of exposure to people in top management. To encourage risk taking among all TRS employees, Gerstner also established something called the Great Performers program to recognize and reward truly exceptional customer service, a central tenet in the organization's vision.

These incentives led quickly to new markets, products, and services. TRS expanded its overseas presence dramatically. By 1988, AmEx cards were issued in 29 currencies (as opposed to only 11 a decade earlier). The unit also focused aggressively on two market segments that had historically received little attention: college students and women. In 1981, TRS combined its card and travel-service capabilities to offer corporate clients a unified system to monitor and control travel expenses. And by 1988, AmEx had grown to become the fifth largest direct-mail merchant in the United States.

Other new products and services included 90-day insurance on all purchases made with the AmEx card, a Platinum American Express card, and a revolving credit card known as Optima. In 1988, the company also switched to image-processing technology for billing, producing a more convenient monthly statement for customers and reducing billing costs by 25%.

As a result of these innovations, TRS's net income increased a phenomenal 500% between 1978 and 1987—a compounded annual rate of about 18%. The business outperformed many so-called high-tech/high-growth companies. With a 1988 return on equity of 28%, it also outperformed most low-growth but high-profit businesses.

stockholders, employees—and how easily it can be translated into a realistic competitive strategy. Bad visions tend to ignore the legitimate needs and rights of important constituencies—favoring, say, employees over customers or stockholders. Or they are strategically unsound. When a company that has never been better than a weak competitor in an industry suddenly starts talking about becoming number one, that is a pipe dream, not a vision.

One of the most frequent mistakes that overmanaged and under-led corporations make is to embrace long-term planning as a panacea for their lack of direction and inability to adapt to an increasingly competitive and dynamic business environment. But such an approach misinterprets the nature of direction setting and can never work.

Long-term planning is always time consuming. Whenever something unexpected happens, plans have to be redone. In a dynamic business environment, the unexpected often becomes the norm, and long-term planning can become an extraordinarily burdensome activity. That is why most successful corporations limit the time frame of their planning activities. Indeed, some even consider "long-term planning" a contradiction in terms.

In a company without direction, even short-term planning can become a black hole capable of absorbing an infinite amount of time and energy. With no vision and strategy to provide constraints around the planning process or to guide it, every eventuality deserves a plan. Under these circumstances, contingency planning can go on forever, draining time and attention from far more essential activities, yet without ever providing the clear sense of direction that a company desperately needs. After awhile, managers inevitably become cynical, and the planning process can degenerate into a highly politicized game.

Planning works best not as a substitute for direction setting but as a complement to it. A competent planning process serves as a useful reality check on direction-setting activities. Likewise, a competent direction-setting process provides a focus in which planning can then be realistically carried out. It helps clarify what kind of planning is essential and what kind is irrelevant.

Aligning People Versus Organizing and Staffing

A central feature of modern organizations is interdependence, where no one has complete autonomy, where most employees are tied to many others by their work, technology, management systems, and hierarchy. These linkages present a special challenge when organizations attempt to change. Unless many individuals line up and move together in the same direction, people will tend to fall all over one another. To executives who are overeducated in management and undereducated in leadership, the idea of getting people moving in the same direction appears to be an organizational problem. What executives need to do, however, is not organize people but align them.

Managers "organize" to create human systems that can implement plans as precisely and efficiently as possible. Typically, this requires a number of potentially complex decisions. A company must choose a structure of jobs and reporting relationships, staff it with individuals suited to the jobs, provide training for those who need it, communicate plans to the workforce, and decide how much authority to delegate and to whom. Economic incentives also need to be constructed to accomplish the plan, as well as systems to monitor its implementation. These organizational judgments are much like architectural decisions. It's a question of fit within a particular context.

Aligning is different. It is more of a communications challenge than a design problem. Aligning invariably involves talking to many more individuals than organizing does. The target population can involve not only a manager's subordinates but also bosses, peers, staff in other parts of the organization, as well as suppliers, government officials, and even customers. Anyone who can help implement the vision and strategies or who can block implementation is relevant.

Trying to get people to comprehend a vision of an alternative future is also a communications challenge of a completely different magnitude from organizing them to fulfill a short-term plan. It's much like the difference between a football quarterback attempting to describe to his team the next two or three plays versus his trying to explain to them a totally new approach to the game to be used in the second half of the season.

Whether delivered with many words or a few carefully chosen symbols, such messages are not necessarily accepted just because they are understood. Another big challenge in leadership efforts is credibility—getting people to believe the message. Many things contribute to credibility: the track record of the person delivering the message, the content of the message itself, the communicator's reputation for integrity and trustworthiness, and the consistency between words and deeds.

Finally, aligning leads to empowerment in a way that organizing rarely does. One of the reasons some organizations have difficulty adjusting to rapid changes in markets or technology is that so many people in those companies feel relatively powerless. They have learned from experience that even if they correctly perceive important external changes and then initiate appropriate actions, they are vulnerable to someone higher up who does not like what they have done. Reprimands can take many different forms: "That's against policy," or "We can't afford it," or "Shut up and do as you're told."

Alignment helps overcome this problem by empowering people in at least two ways. First, when a clear sense of direction has been communicated throughout an organization, lower-level employees can initiate actions without the same degree of vulnerability. As long as their behavior is consistent with the vision, superiors will have more difficulty reprimanding them. Second, because everyone is aiming at the same target, the probability is less that one person's initiative will be stalled when it comes into conflict with someone else's.

Motivating People Versus Controlling and Problem Solving

Since change is the function of leadership, being able to generate highly energized behavior is important for coping with the inevitable barriers to change. Just as direction setting identifies an appropriate path for movement and just as effective alignment gets people moving down that path, successful motivation ensures that they will have the energy to overcome obstacles.

According to the logic of management, control mechanisms compare system behavior with the plan and take action when a deviation is detected. In a well-managed factory, for example, this means the planning process establishes sensible quality targets, the organizing process builds an organization that can achieve those targets, and a control process makes sure that quality lapses are spotted immediately, not in 30 or 60 days, and corrected.

For some of the same reasons that control is so central to management, highly motivated or inspired behavior is almost irrelevant. Managerial processes must be as close as possible to fail-safe and risk free. That means they cannot be dependent on the unusual or hard to obtain. The whole purpose of systems and structures is to help normal people who behave in normal ways to complete routine jobs successfully, day after day. It's not exciting or glamorous. But that's management.

Leadership is different. Achieving grand visions always requires a burst of energy. Motivation and inspiration energize people, not by pushing them in the right direction as control mechanisms do but by satisfying basic human needs for achievement, a sense of belonging, recognition, self-esteem, a feeling of control over one's life, and the ability to live up to one's ideals. Such feelings touch us deeply and elicit a powerful response.

Good leaders motivate people in a variety of ways. First, they always articulate the organization's vision in a manner that stresses the values of the audience they are addressing. This makes the work important to those individuals. Leaders also regularly involve people in deciding how to achieve the organization's vision (or the part most relevant to a particular individual). This gives people a sense of control. Another important motivational technique is to support employee efforts to realize the vision by providing coaching, feedback, and role modeling, thereby helping people grow professionally and enhancing their self-esteem. Finally, good leaders recognize and reward success, which not only gives people a sense of accomplishment but also makes them feel like they belong to an organization that cares about them. When all this is done, the work itself becomes intrinsically motivating.

The more that change characterizes the business environment, the more that leaders must motivate people to provide leadership as well. When this works, it tends to reproduce leadership across the

Motivating People: Richard Nicolosi at Procter and Gamble

FOR ABOUT 20 YEARS AFTER ITS FOUNDING in 1956, Procter & Gamble's paper products division had experienced little competition for its high-quality, reasonably priced, and well-marketed consumer goods. By the late 1970s, however, the market position of the division had changed. New competitive thrusts hurt P&G badly. For example, industry analysts estimate that the company's market share for disposable diapers fell from 75% in the mid-1970s to 52% in 1984.

That year, Richard Nicolosi came to paper products as the associate general manager, after three years in P&G's smaller and faster moving soft-drink business. He found a heavily bureaucratic and centralized organization that was overly preoccupied with internal functional goals and projects. Almost all information about customers came through highly quantitative market research. The technical people were rewarded for cost savings, the commercial people focused on volume and share, and the two groups were nearly at war with each other.

During the late summer of 1984, top management announced that Nicolosi would become the head of paper products in October, and by August he was unofficially running the division. Immediately he began to stress the need for the division to become more creative and market driven, instead of just trying to be a low-cost producer. "I had to make it very clear," Nicolosi later reported, "that the rules of the game had changed."

The new direction included a much greater stress on teamwork and multiple leadership roles. Nicolosi pushed a strategy of using groups to manage the division and its specific products. In October, he and his team designated themselves as the paper division "board" and began meeting first monthly and then weekly. In November, they established "category teams" to manage their major brand groups (like diapers, tissues, towels) and started pushing responsibility down to these teams. "Shun the incremental," Nicolosi stressed, "and go for the leap."

In December, Nicolosi selectively involved himself in more detail in certain activities. He met with the advertising agency and got to know key creative people. He asked the marketing manager of diapers to report directly to him, eliminating a layer in the hierarchy. He talked more to the people who were working on new product development projects.

In January 1985, the board announced a new organizational structure that included not only category teams but also new-brand business teams. By the spring, the board was ready to plan an important motivational event to communicate the new paper products vision to as many people as possible. On June 4, 1985, all the Cincinnati-based personnel in paper plus sales district managers and paper plant managers—several thousand people in all—met in the local Masonic Temple. Nicolosi and other board members described their vision of an organization where "each of us is a leader." The event was videotaped, and an edited version was sent to all sales offices and plants for everyone to see.

All these activities helped create an entrepreneurial environment where large numbers of people were motivated to realize the new vision. Most innovations came from people dealing with new products. Ultra Pampers, first introduced in February 1985, took the market share of the entire Pampers product line from 40% to 58% and profitability from break-even to positive. And within only a few months of the introduction of Luvs Delux in May 1987, market share for the overall brand grew by 150%.

Other employee initiatives were oriented more toward a functional area, and some came from the bottom of the hierarchy. In the spring of 1986, a few of the division's secretaries, feeling empowered by the new culture, developed a secretaries network. This association established subcommittees on training, on rewards and recognition, and on the "secretary of the future." Echoing the sentiments of many of her peers, one paper products secretary said: "I don't see why we, too, can't contribute to the division's new direction."

By the end of 1988, revenues at the paper products division were up 40% over a four-year period. Profits were up 68%. And this happened despite the fact that the competition continued to get tougher.

entire organization, with people occupying multiple leadership roles throughout the hierarchy. This is highly valuable, because coping with change in any complex business demands initiatives from a multitude of people. Nothing less will work.

Of course, leadership from many sources does not necessarily converge. To the contrary, it can easily conflict. For multiple leadership roles to work together, people's actions must be carefully coordinated by mechanisms that differ from those coordinating traditional management roles.

Strong networks of informal relationships—the kind found in companies with healthy cultures—help coordinate leadership activities in much the same way that formal structure coordinates managerial activities. The key difference is that informal networks can deal with the greater demands for coordination associated with nonroutine activities and change. The multitude of communication channels and the trust among the individuals connected by those channels allow for an ongoing process of accommodation and adaptation. When conflicts arise among roles, those same relationships help resolve the conflicts. Perhaps most important, this process of dialogue and accommodation can produce visions that are linked and compatible instead of remote and competitive. All this requires a great deal more communication than is needed to coordinate managerial roles, but unlike formal structure, strong informal networks can handle it.

Informal relations of some sort exist in all corporations. But too often these networks are either very weak—some people are well connected but most are not—or they are highly fragmented—a strong network exists inside the marketing group and inside R&D but not across the two departments. Such networks do not support multiple leadership initiatives well. In fact, extensive informal networks are so important that if they do not exist, creating them has to be the focus of activity early in a major leadership initiative.

Creating a Culture of Leadership

Despite the increasing importance of leadership to business success, the on-the-job experiences of most people actually seem to undermine the development of the attributes needed for leadership. Nevertheless, some companies have consistently demonstrated an ability to develop people into outstanding leader-managers. Recruiting people with leadership potential is only the first step. Equally important is managing their career patterns. Individuals who are effective in large leadership roles often share a number of career experiences.

Perhaps the most typical and most important is significant challenge early in a career. Leaders almost always have had opportunities during their twenties and thirties to actually try to lead, to take a risk, and to learn from both triumphs and failures. Such learning seems essential in developing a wide range of leadership skills and perspectives. These opportunities also teach people something about both the difficulty of leadership and its potential for producing change.

Later in their careers, something equally important happens that has to do with broadening. People who provide effective leadership in important jobs always have a chance, before they get into those jobs, to grow beyond the narrow base that characterizes most managerial careers. This is usually the result of lateral career moves or of early promotions to unusually broad job assignments. Sometimes other vehicles help, like special task-force assignments or a lengthy general management course. Whatever the case, the breadth of knowledge developed in this way seems to be helpful in all aspects of leadership. So does the network of relationships that is often acquired both inside and outside the company. When enough people get opportunities like this, the relationships that are built also help create the strong informal networks needed to support multiple leadership initiatives.

Corporations that do a better-than-average job of developing leaders put an emphasis on creating challenging opportunities for relatively young employees. In many businesses, decentralization is the key. By definition, it pushes responsibility lower in an organization and in the process creates more challenging jobs at lower levels. Johnson & Johnson, 3M, Hewlett-Packard, General Electric, and many other well-known companies have used that approach quite successfully. Some of those same companies also create as many small units as possible so there are a lot of challenging lower-level general management jobs available.

Sometimes these businesses develop additional challenging opportunities by stressing growth through new products or services. Over the years, 3M has had a policy that at least 25% of its revenue should come from products introduced within the last five years. That encourages small new ventures, which in turn offer hundreds of opportunities to test and stretch young people with leadership potential.

Such practices can, almost by themselves, prepare people for small- and medium-sized leadership jobs. But developing people for important leadership positions requires more work on the part of senior executives, often over a long period of time. That work begins with efforts to spot people with great leadership potential early in their careers and to identify what will be needed to stretch and develop them.

Again, there is nothing magic about this process. The methods successful companies use are surprisingly straightforward. They go out of their way to make young employees and people at lower levels in their organizations visible to senior management. Senior managers then judge for themselves who has potential and what the development needs of those people are. Executives also discuss their tentative conclusions among themselves to draw more accurate judgments.

Armed with a clear sense of who has considerable leadership potential and what skills they need to develop, executives in these companies then spend time planning for that development. Sometimes that is done as part of a formal succession planning or high-potential development process; often it is more informal. In either case, the key ingredient appears to be an intelligent assessment of what feasible development opportunities fit each candidate's needs.

To encourage managers to participate in these activities, well-led businesses tend to recognize and reward people who successfully develop leaders. This is rarely done as part of a formal compensation or bonus formula, simply because it is so difficult to measure such achievements with precision. But it does become a factor in decisions about promotion, especially to the most senior levels, and that seems to make a big difference. When told that future promotions will depend to some degree on their ability to nurture leaders, even people who say that leadership cannot be developed somehow find ways to do it.

Such strategies help create a corporate culture where people value strong leadership and strive to create it. Just as we need more people to provide leadership in the complex organizations that dominate our world today, we also need more people to develop the cultures that will create that leadership. Institutionalizing a leadership-centered culture is the ultimate act of leadership.

Originally published May 1990. Reprint R0111F

The Work of Leadership

by Ronald A. Heifetz and Donald L. Laurie

TO STAY ALIVE, JACK PRITCHARD had to change his life. Triple bypass surgery and medication could help, the heart surgeon told him, but no technical fix could release Pritchard from his own responsibility for changing the habits of a lifetime. He had to stop smoking, improve his diet, get some exercise, and take time to relax, remembering to breathe more deeply each day. Pritchard's doctor could provide sustaining technical expertise and take supportive action, but only Pritchard could adapt his ingrained habits to improve his long-term health. The doctor faced the leadership task of mobilizing the patient to make critical behavioral changes; Jack Pritchard faced the adaptive work of figuring out which specific changes to make and how to incorporate them into his daily life.

Companies today face challenges similar to the ones that confronted Pritchard and his doctor. They face adaptive challenges. Changes in societies, markets, customers, competition, and technology around the globe are forcing organizations to clarify their values, develop new strategies, and learn new ways of operating. Often the toughest task for leaders in effecting change is mobilizing people throughout the organization to do adaptive work.

Adaptive work is required when our deeply held beliefs are challenged, when the values that made us successful become less relevant, and when legitimate yet competing perspectives emerge. We see adaptive challenges every day at every level of the workplace—when companies restructure or reengineer, develop or implement strategy, or merge businesses. We see adaptive challenges when marketing has difficulty working with operations, when cross-functional teams don't work well, or when senior executives complain, "We don't seem to be able to execute effectively." Adaptive problems are often systemic problems with no ready answers.

Mobilizing an organization to adapt its behaviors in order to thrive in new business environments is critical. Without such change, any company today would falter. Indeed, getting people to do adaptive work is the mark of leadership in a competitive world. Yet for most senior executives, providing leadership and not just authoritative expertise is extremely difficult. Why? We see two reasons. First, in order to make change happen, executives have to break a long-standing behavior pattern of their own: providing leadership in the form of solutions. This tendency is quite natural because many executives reach their positions of authority by virtue of their competence in taking responsibility and solving problems. But the locus of responsibility for problem solving when a company faces an adaptive challenge must shift to its people. Solutions to adaptive challenges reside not in the executive suite but in the collective intelligence of employees at all levels, who need to use one another as resources, often across boundaries, and learn their way to those solutions.

Second, adaptive change is distressing for the people going through it. They need to take on new roles, new relationships, new values, new behaviors, and new approaches to work. Many employees are ambivalent about the efforts and sacrifices required of them. They often look to the senior executive to take problems off their shoulders. But those expectations have to be unlearned. Rather than fulfilling the expectation that they will provide answers, leaders have to ask tough questions. Rather than protecting people from outside threats, leaders should allow them to feel the pinch of reality in order to stimulate them to adapt. Instead of orienting people to their current roles, leaders must disorient them so that new relationships can develop. Instead of quelling conflict, leaders have to draw

Idea in Brief

What presents your company with its toughest challenges? Shifting markets? Stiffening competition? Emerging technologies? When such challenges intensify, you may need to reclarify corporate values, redesign strategies, merge or dissolve businesses, or manage cross-functional strife.

These **adaptive challenges** are murky, systemic problems with no easy answers. Perhaps even more vexing, the solutions to adaptive challenges *don't* reside in the executive suite. Solving them requires the involvement of people *throughout* your organization.

Adaptive work is tough on everyone. For *leaders*, it's counterintuitive.

Rather than providing solutions, you must ask tough questions and leverage employees' collective intelligence. Instead of maintaining norms, you must challenge the "way we do business." And rather than quelling conflict, you need to draw issues out and let people feel the sting of reality.

For your *employees*, adaptive work is painful—requiring unfamiliar roles, responsibilities, values, and ways of working. No wonder employees often try to lob adaptive work back to their leaders.

How to ensure that you *and* your employees embrace the challenges of adaptive work? Applying the following six principles will help.

the issues out. Instead of maintaining norms, leaders have to challenge "the way we do business" and help others distinguish immutable values from historical practices that must go.

Drawing on our experience with managers from around the world, we offer six principles for leading adaptive work: "getting on the balcony," identifying the adaptive challenge, regulating distress, maintaining disciplined attention, giving the work back to people, and protecting voices of leadership from below. We illustrate those principles with an example of adaptive change at KPMG Netherlands, a professional-services firm.

Get on the Balcony

Earvin "Magic" Johnson's greatness in leading his basketball team came in part from his ability to play hard while keeping the whole game situation in mind, as if he stood in a press box or on a balcony

Idea in Practice

1. Get on the balcony. Don't get swept up in the field of play. Instead, move back and forth between the "action" and the "balcony." You'll spot emerging patterns, such as power struggles or work avoidance. This high-level perspective helps you mobilize people to do adaptive work.

2. Identify your adaptive challenge.

Example: When British Airways' passengers nicknamed it "Bloody Awful," CEO Colin Marshall knew he had to infuse the company with a dedication to customers. He identified the adaptive challenge as "creating trust throughout British Airways." To diagnose the challenge further, Marshall's team mingled with employees and customers in baggage areas, reservation centers, and planes, asking which beliefs, values, and behaviors needed overhauling. They exposed value-based conflicts underlying surface-level disputes, and resolved the team's own dysfunctional conflicts that impaired companywide collaboration. By understanding themselves, their people, and the company's conflicts, the team strengthened British Airways' bid to become "the World's Favourite Airline."

3. Regulate distress. To inspire change—without disabling people—pace adaptive work:

above the field of play. Bobby Orr played hockey in the same way. Other players might fail to recognize the larger patterns of play that performers like Johnson and Orr quickly understand, because they are so engaged in the game that they get carried away by it. Their attention is captured by the rapid motion, the physical contact, the roar of the crowd, and the pressure to execute. In sports, most players simply may not see who is open for a pass, who is missing a block, or how the offense and defense work together. Players like Johnson and Orr watch these things and allow their observations to guide their actions.

Business leaders have to be able to view patterns as if they were on a balcony. It does them no good to be swept up in the field of action. Leaders have to see a context for change or create one. They should give employees a strong sense of the history of the enterprise

- First, let employees debate issues and clarify assumptions behind competing views—safely.

- Then provide direction. Define *key* issues and values. Control the rate of change: Don't start too many initiatives simultaneously without stopping others.

- Maintain just enough tension, resisting pressure to restore the status quo. Raise tough questions without succumbing to anxiety yourself. Communicate presence and poise.

4. Maintain disciplined attention. Encourage managers to grapple with divisive issues, rather than indulging in scapegoating or denial. Deepen the debate to unlock polarized, superficial conflict. Demonstrate collaboration to solve problems.

5. Give the work back to employees. To instill collective self-confidence—versus dependence on you—support rather than control people. Encourage risk-taking and responsibility—then back people up if they err. Help them recognize they contain the solutions.

6. Protect leadership voices from below. Don't silence whistle-blowers, creative deviants, and others exposing contradictions within your company. Their perspectives can provoke fresh thinking. Ask, "What is this guy *really* talking about? Have we missed something?"

and what's good about its past, as well as an idea of the market forces at work today and the responsibility people must take in shaping the future. Leaders must be able to identify struggles over values and power, recognize patterns of work avoidance, and watch for the many other functional and dysfunctional reactions to change.

Without the capacity to move back and forth between the field of action and the balcony, to reflect day to day, moment to moment, on the many ways in which an organization's habits can sabotage adaptive work, a leader easily and unwittingly becomes a prisoner of the system. The dynamics of adaptive change are far too complex to keep track of, let alone influence, if leaders stay only on the field of play.

We have encountered several leaders, some of whom we discuss in this article, who manage to spend much of their precious time on the balcony as they guide their organizations through change.

Without that perspective, they probably would have been unable to mobilize people to do adaptive work. Getting on the balcony is thus a prerequisite for following the next five principles.

Identify the Adaptive Challenge

When a leopard threatens a band of chimpanzees, the leopard rarely succeeds in picking off a stray. Chimps know how to respond to this kind of threat. But when a man with an automatic rifle comes near, the routine responses fail. Chimps risk extinction in a world of poachers unless they figure out how to disarm the new threat. Similarly, when businesses cannot learn quickly to adapt to new challenges, they are likely to face their own form of extinction.

Consider the well-known case of British Airways. Having observed the revolutionary changes in the airline industry during the 1980s, then chief executive Colin Marshall clearly recognized the need to transform an airline nicknamed Bloody Awful by its own passengers into an exemplar of customer service. He also understood that this ambition would require more than anything else changes in values, practices, and relationships throughout the company. An organization whose people clung to functional silos and valued pleasing their bosses more than pleasing customers could not become "the world's favorite airline." Marshall needed an organization dedicated to serving people, acting on trust, respecting the individual, and making teamwork happen across boundaries. Values had to change throughout British Airways. People had to learn to collaborate and to develop a collective sense of responsibility for the direction and performance of the airline. Marshall identified the essential adaptive challenge: creating trust throughout the organization. He is one of the first executives we have known to make "creating trust" a priority.

To lead British Airways, Marshall had to get his executive team to understand the nature of the threat created by dissatisfied customers: Did it represent a technical challenge or an adaptive challenge? Would expert advice and technical adjustments within basic routines suffice, or would people throughout the company have to learn different ways of doing business, develop new competencies, and begin to work collectively?

Marshall and his team set out to diagnose in more detail the organization's challenges. They looked in three places. First, they listened to the ideas and concerns of people inside and outside the organization—meeting with crews on flights, showing up in the 350-person reservations center in New York, wandering around the baggage-handling area in Tokyo, or visiting the passenger lounge in whatever airport they happened to be in. Their primary questions were, Whose values, beliefs, attitudes, or behaviors would have to change in order for progress to take place? What shifts in priorities, resources, and power were necessary? What sacrifices would have to be made and by whom?

Second, Marshall and his team saw conflicts as clues—symptoms of adaptive challenges. The way conflicts across functions were being expressed were mere surface phenomena; the underlying conflicts had to be diagnosed. Disputes over seemingly technical issues such as procedures, schedules, and lines of authority were in fact proxies for underlying conflicts about values and norms.

Third, Marshall and his team held a mirror up to themselves, recognizing that they embodied the adaptive challenges facing the organization. Early in the transformation of British Airways, competing values and norms were played out on the executive team in dysfunctional ways that impaired the capacity of the rest of the company to collaborate across functions and units and make the necessary trade-offs. No executive can hide from the fact that his or her team reflects the best and the worst of the company's values and norms, and therefore provides a case in point for insight into the nature of the adaptive work ahead.

Thus, identifying its adaptive challenge was crucial in British Airways' bid to become the world's favorite airline. For the strategy to succeed, the company's leaders needed to understand themselves, their people, and the potential sources of conflict. Marshall recognized that strategy development itself requires adaptive work.

Regulate Distress

Adaptive work generates distress. Before putting people to work on challenges for which there are no ready solutions, a leader must realize that people can learn only so much so fast. At the same time, they must feel the need to change as reality brings new challenges. They cannot learn new ways when they are overwhelmed, but eliminating stress altogether removes the impetus for doing adaptive work. Because a leader must strike a delicate balance between having people feel the need to change and having them feel overwhelmed by change, leadership is a razor's edge.

A leader must attend to three fundamental tasks in order to help maintain a productive level of tension. Adhering to these tasks will allow him or her to motivate people without disabling them. First, a leader must create what can be called a *holding environment*. To use the analogy of a pressure cooker, a leader needs to regulate the pressure by turning up the heat while also allowing some steam to escape. If the pressure exceeds the cooker's capacity, the cooker can blow up. However, nothing cooks without some heat.

In the early stages of a corporate change, the holding environment can be a temporary "place" in which a leader creates the conditions for diverse groups to talk to one another about the challenges facing them, to frame and debate issues, and to clarify the assumptions behind competing perspectives and values. Over time, more issues can be phased in as they become ripe. At British Airways, for example, the shift from an internal focus to a customer focus took place over four or five years and dealt with important issues in succession: building a credible executive team, communicating with a highly fragmented organization, defining new measures of performance and compensation, and developing sophisticated information systems. During that time, employees at all levels learned to identify what and how they needed to change.

Thus, a leader must sequence and pace the work. Too often, senior managers convey that everything is important. They start new initiatives without stopping other activities, or they start too many initiatives at the same time. They overwhelm and disorient the very people who need to take responsibility for the work.

Second, a leader is responsible for direction, protection, orientation, managing conflict, and shaping norms. (See the exhibit "Adaptive Work Calls for Leadership.") Fulfilling these responsibilities is also important for a manager in technical or routine situations. But a leader engaged in adaptive work uses his authority to fulfill them differently. A leader provides direction by identifying the organization's adaptive challenge and framing the key questions and issues. A leader protects people by managing the rate of change. A leader orients people to new roles and responsibilities by clarifying business realities and key values. A leader helps expose conflict, viewing it as the engine of creativity and learning. Finally, a leader helps the organization maintain those norms that must endure and challenge those that need to change.

Adaptive work calls for leadership

In the course of regulating people's distress, a leader faces several key responsibilities and may have to use his or her authority differently depending on the type of work situation.

Leader's responsibilities	Type of situation	
	Technical or routine	*Adaptive*
Direction	Define problems and provide solutions	Identify the adaptive challenge and frame key questions and issues
Protection	Shield the organization from external threats	Let the organization feel external pressures within a range it can stand
Orientation	Clarify roles and responsibilities	Challenge current roles and resist pressure to define new roles quickly
Managing conflict	Restore order	Expose conflict or let it emerge
Shaping norms	Maintain norms	Challenge unproductive norms

65

Third, a leader must have presence and poise; regulating distress is perhaps a leader's most difficult job. The pressures to restore equilibrium are enormous. Just as molecules bang hard against the walls of a pressure cooker, people bang up against leaders who are trying to sustain the pressures of tough, conflict-filled work. Although leadership demands a deep understanding of the pain of change—the fears and sacrifices associated with major readjustment—it also requires the ability to hold steady and maintain the tension. Otherwise, the pressure escapes and the stimulus for learning and change is lost.

A leader has to have the emotional capacity to tolerate uncertainty, frustration, and pain. He has to be able to raise tough questions without getting too anxious himself. Employees as well as colleagues and customers will carefully observe verbal and nonverbal cues to a leader's ability to hold steady. He needs to communicate confidence that he and they can tackle the tasks ahead.

Maintain Disciplined Attention

Different people within the same organization bring different experiences, assumptions, values, beliefs, and habits to their work. This diversity is valuable because innovation and learning are the products of differences. No one learns anything without being open to contrasting points of view. Yet managers at all levels are often unwilling—or unable—to address their competing perspectives collectively. They frequently avoid paying attention to issues that disturb them. They restore equilibrium quickly, often with work avoidance maneuvers. A leader must get employees to confront tough trade-offs in values, procedures, operating styles, and power.

That is as true at the top of the organization as it is in the middle or on the front line. Indeed, if the executive team cannot model adaptive work, the organization will languish. If senior managers can't draw out and deal with divisive issues, how will people elsewhere in the organization change their behaviors and rework their relationships? As Jan Carlzon, the legendary CEO of Scandinavian Airlines System (SAS), told us, "One of the most interesting missions of leadership is getting people on the executive team to listen to and learn from one another. Held in debate, people can learn their way to collective solutions when they understand one another's assumptions. The work of the leader is to get conflict out into the open and use it as a source of creativity."

Because work avoidance is rampant in organizations, a leader has to counteract distractions that prevent people from dealing with adaptive issues. Scapegoating, denial, focusing only on today's technical issues, or attacking individuals rather than the perspectives they represent—all forms of work avoidance—are to be expected when an organization undertakes adaptive work. Distractions have to be identified when they occur so that people will regain focus.

When sterile conflict takes the place of dialogue, a leader has to step in and put the team to work on reframing the issues. She has to deepen the debate with questions, unbundling the issues into their parts rather than letting conflict remain polarized and superficial. When people preoccupy themselves with blaming external forces, higher management, or a heavy workload, a leader has to sharpen the team's sense of responsibility for carving out the time to press forward. When the team fragments and individuals resort to protecting their own turf, leaders have to demonstrate the need for collaboration. People have to discover the value of consulting with one another and using one another as resources in the problem-solving process. For example, one CEO we know uses executive meetings, even those that focus on operational and technical issues, as opportunities to teach the team how to work collectively on adaptive problems.

Of course, only the rare manager intends to avoid adaptive work. In general, people feel ambivalent about it. Although they want to make progress on hard problems or live up to their renewed and clarified values, people also want to avoid the associated distress. Just as millions of U.S. citizens want to reduce the federal budget deficit, but not by giving up their tax dollars or benefits or jobs, so, too, managers may consider adaptive work a priority but have difficulty sacrificing their familiar ways of doing business. People need leadership to help them maintain their focus on the tough questions. Disciplined attention is the currency of leadership.

Give the Work Back to People

Everyone in the organization has special access to information that comes from his or her particular vantage point. Everyone may see different needs and opportunities. People who sense early changes in the marketplace are often at the periphery, but the organization will thrive if it can bring that information to bear on tactical and strategic decisions. When people do not act on their special knowledge, businesses fail to adapt.

All too often, people look up the chain of command, expecting senior management to meet market challenges for which they themselves are responsible. Indeed, the greater and more persistent distresses that accompany adaptive work make such dependence worse. People tend to become passive, and senior managers who pride themselves on being problem solvers take decisive action. That behavior restores equilibrium in the short term but ultimately leads to complacency and habits of work avoidance that shield people from responsibility, pain, and the need to change.

Getting people to assume greater responsibility is not easy. Not only are many lower-level employees comfortable being told what to do, but many managers are accustomed to treating subordinates like machinery that requires control. Letting people take the initiative in defining and solving problems means that management needs to learn to support rather than control. Workers, for their part, need to learn to take responsibility.

Jan Carlzon encouraged responsibility taking at SAS by trusting others and decentralizing authority. A leader has to let people bear the weight of responsibility. "The key is to let them discover the problem," he said. "You won't be successful if people aren't carrying the recognition of the problem and the solution within themselves." To that end, Carlzon sought widespread engagement.

For example, in his first two years at SAS, Carlzon spent up to 50% of his time communicating directly in large meetings and indirectly in a host of innovative ways: through workshops, brainstorming sessions, learning exercises, newsletters, brochures, and exposure in the public media. He demonstrated through a variety of symbolic acts—for example, by eliminating the pretentious executive dining room and burning thousands of pages of manuals and handbooks—the extent to which rules had come to dominate the company. He made himself a pervasive presence, meeting with and listening to people both inside and outside the organization. He even wrote a book, *Moments of Truth* (HarperCollins, 1989), to explain his values, philosophy, and strategy. As Carlzon noted, "If no one else read it, at least my people would."

A leader also must develop collective self-confidence. Again, Carlzon said it well: "People aren't born with self-confidence. Even the most self-confident people can be broken. Self-confidence comes from success, experience, and the organization's environment. The leader's most important role is to instill confidence in people. They must dare to take risks and responsibility. You must back them up if they make mistakes."

Protect Voices of Leadership from Below

Giving a voice to all people is the foundation of an organization that is willing to experiment and learn. But, in fact, whistle-blowers, creative deviants, and other such original voices routinely get smashed and silenced in organizational life. They generate disequilibrium, and the easiest way for an organization to restore equilibrium is to neutralize those voices, sometimes in the name of teamwork and "alignment."

The voices from below are usually not as articulate as one would wish. People speaking beyond their authority usually feel self-conscious and sometimes have to generate "too much" passion to get themselves geared up for speaking out. Of course, that often makes it harder for them to communicate effectively. They pick the wrong time and place, and often bypass proper channels of communication and lines of authority. But buried inside a poorly packaged interjection may lie an important intuition that needs to be teased out and considered. To toss it out for its bad timing, lack of clarity, or seeming unreasonableness is to lose potentially valuable information and discourage a potential leader in the organization.

That is what happened to David, a manager in a large manufacturing company. He had listened when his superiors encouraged people to look for problems, speak openly, and take responsibility. So he raised an issue about one of the CEO's pet projects—an issue that was deemed "too hot to handle" and had been swept under the carpet for years. Everyone understood that it was not open to discussion, but David knew that proceeding with the project could damage or derail key elements of the company's overall strategy. He raised the issue directly in a meeting with his boss and the CEO. He provided a clear description of the problem, a rundown of competing perspectives, and a summary of the consequences of continuing to pursue the project.

The CEO angrily squelched the discussion and reinforced the positive aspects of his pet project. When David and his boss left the room, his boss exploded: "Who do you think you are, with your holier-than-thou attitude?" He insinuated that David had never liked the CEO's pet project because David hadn't come up with the idea himself. The subject was closed.

David had greater expertise in the area of the project than either his boss or the CEO. But his two superiors demonstrated no curiosity, no effort to investigate David's reasoning, no awareness that he was behaving responsibly with the interests of the company at heart. It rapidly became clear to David that it was more important to understand what mattered to the boss than to focus on real issues. The CEO and David's boss together squashed the viewpoint of a leader from below and thereby killed his potential for leadership in the organization. He would either leave the company or never go against the grain again.

Leaders must rely on others within the business to raise questions that may indicate an impending adaptive challenge. They have to provide cover to people who point to the internal contradictions of the enterprise. Those individuals often have the perspective to provoke rethinking that people in authority do not. Thus, as a rule of thumb, when authority figures feel the reflexive urge to glare at or otherwise silence someone, they should resist. The urge to restore social equilibrium is quite powerful, and it comes on fast. One has to get accustomed to getting on the balcony, delaying the impulse, and asking, What is this guy really talking about? Is there something we're missing?

Doing Adaptive Work at KPMG Netherlands

The highly successful KPMG Netherlands provides a good example of how a company can engage in adaptive work. In 1994, Ruud Koedijk, the firm's chairman, recognized a strategic challenge. Although the auditing, consulting, and tax-preparation partnership was the industry leader in the Netherlands and was highly profitable, growth opportunities in the segments it served were limited. Margins in the auditing business were being squeezed as the market became more saturated, and competition in the consulting business was increasing as well. Koedijk knew that the firm needed to move into more profitable growth areas, but he didn't know what they were or how KPMG might identify them.

Koedijk and his board were confident that they had the tools to do the analytical strategy work: analyze trends and discontinuities, understand core competencies, assess their competitive position, and map potential opportunities. They were considerably less certain that they could commit to implementing the strategy that would emerge from their work. Historically, the partnership had resisted attempts to change, basically because the partners were content with the way things were. They had been successful for a long time, so they saw no reason to learn new ways of doing business, either from their fellow partners or from anyone lower down in the organization. Overturning the partners' attitude and its deep impact on the organization's culture posed an enormous adaptive challenge for KPMG.

Koedijk could see from the balcony that the very structure of KPMG inhibited change. In truth, KPMG was less a partnership than a collection of small fiefdoms in which each partner was a lord. The firm's success was the cumulative accomplishment of each of the individual partners, not the unified result of 300 colleagues pulling together toward a shared ambition. Success was measured solely in terms of the profitability of individual units. As one partner described it, "If the bottom line was correct, you were a 'good fellow.'" As a result, one partner would not trespass on another's turf, and learning from others was a rare event. Because independence was so highly valued, confrontations were rare and conflict was camouflaged. If partners wanted to resist firmwide change, they did not kill the issue directly. "Say yes, do no" was the operative phrase.

Koedijk also knew that this sense of autonomy got in the way of developing new talent at KPMG. Directors rewarded their subordinates for two things: not making mistakes and delivering a high number of billable hours per week. The emphasis was not on creativity or innovation. Partners were looking for errors when they reviewed their subordinates' work, not for new understanding or fresh insight. Although Koedijk could see the broad outlines of the adaptive challenges facing his organization, he knew that he could not mandate behavioral change. What he could do was create the conditions for people to discover for themselves how they needed to change. He set a process in motion to make that happen.

To start, Koedijk held a meeting of all 300 partners and focused their attention on the history of KPMG, the current business reality, and the business issues they could expect to face. He then raised the question of how they would go about changing as a firm and asked for their perspectives on the issues. By launching the strategic initiative through dialogue rather than edict, he built trust within the partner ranks. Based on this emerging trust and his own credibility, Koedijk persuaded the partners to release 100 partners and nonpartners from their day-to-day responsibilities to work on the strategic challenges. They would devote 60% of their time for nearly four months to that work.

Koedijk and his colleagues established a strategic integration team of 12 senior partners to work with the 100 professionals (called "the 100") from different levels and disciplines. Engaging people below the rank of partner in a major strategic initiative was unheard of and signaled a new approach from the start: Many of these people's opinions had never before been valued or sought by authority figures in the firm. Divided into 14 task forces, the 100 were to work in three areas: gauging future trends and discontinuities, defining core competencies, and grappling with the adaptive challenges facing the organization. They were housed on a separate floor with their own support staff, and they were unfettered by traditional rules and regulations. Hennie Both, KPMG's director of marketing and communications, signed on as project manager.

As the strategy work got under way, the task forces had to confront the existing KPMG culture. Why? Because they literally could not do their new work within the old rules. They could not work when strong respect for the individual came at the expense of effective teamwork, when deeply held individual beliefs got in the way of genuine discussion, and when unit loyalties formed a barrier to cross-functional problem solving. Worst of all, task force members found themselves avoiding conflict and unable to discuss those problems. A number of the task forces became dysfunctional and unable to do their strategy work.

To focus their attention on what needed to change, Both helped the task forces map the culture they desired against the current culture. They discovered very little overlap. The top descriptors of the current culture were: develop opposing views, demand perfection, and avoid conflict. The top characteristics of the desired culture were: create the opportunity for self-fulfillment, develop a caring environment, and maintain trusting relations with colleagues. Articulating this gap made tangible for the group the adaptive challenge that Koedijk saw facing KPMG. In other words, the people who needed to do the changing had finally framed the adaptive challenge for themselves: How could KPMG succeed at a competence-based strategy that depended on cooperation across multiple units and layers if its people couldn't succeed in these task forces? Armed with that understanding, the task force members could become emissaries to the rest of the firm.

On a more personal level, each member was asked to identify his or her individual adaptive challenge. What attitudes, behaviors, or habits did each one need to change, and what specific actions would he or she take? Who else needed to be involved for individual change to take root? Acting as coaches and consultants, the task force members gave one another supportive feedback and suggestions. They had learned to confide, to listen, and to advise with genuine care.

Progress on these issues raised the level of trust dramatically, and task force members began to understand what adapting their behavior meant in everyday terms. They understood how to identify an adaptive issue and developed a language with which to discuss what they needed to do to improve their collective ability to solve problems. They talked about dialogue, work avoidance, and using the collective intelligence of the group. They knew how to call one another on dysfunctional behavior. They had begun to develop the culture required to implement the new business strategy.

Despite the critical breakthroughs toward developing a collective understanding of the adaptive challenge, regulating the level of distress was a constant preoccupation for Koedijk, the board, and Both. The nature of the work was distressing. Strategy work means broad assignments with limited instructions; at KPMG, people were accustomed to highly structured assignments. Strategy work also means being creative. At one breakfast meeting, a board member stood on a table to challenge the group to be more creative and toss aside old rules. This radical and unexpected behavior further raised the distress level: No one had ever seen a partner behave this way before. People realized that their work experience had prepared them only for performing routine tasks with people "like them" from their own units.

The process allowed for conflict and focused people's attention on the hot issues in order to help them learn how to work with conflict in a constructive manner. But the heat was kept within a tolerable range in some of the following ways:

- On one occasion when tensions were unusually high, the 100 were brought together to voice their concerns to the board in an Oprah Winfrey–style meeting. The board sat in the center of an auditorium and took pointed questions from the surrounding group.

- The group devised sanctions to discourage unwanted behavior. In the soccer-crazy Netherlands, all participants in the process were issued the yellow cards that soccer referees use to indicate "foul" to offending players. They used the cards to stop the action when someone started arguing his or her point without listening to or understanding the assumptions and competing perspectives of other participants.

- The group created symbols. They compared the old KPMG to a hippopotamus that was large and cumbersome, liked to sleep a lot, and became aggressive when its normal habits were disturbed. They aspired to be dolphins, which they characterized as playful, eager to learn, and happily willing to go the extra mile for the team. They even paid attention to the statement that clothes make: It surprised some clients to see managers wandering through the KPMG offices that summer in Bermuda shorts and T-shirts.

- The group made a deliberate point of having fun. "Playtime" could mean long bicycle rides or laser-gun games at a local amusement center. In one spontaneous moment at the KPMG offices, a discussion of the power of people mobilized toward a common goal led the group to go outside and use their collective leverage to move a seemingly immovable concrete block.

- The group attended frequent two- and three-day off-site meetings to help bring closure to parts of the work.

These actions, taken as a whole, altered attitudes and behaviors. Curiosity became more valued than obedience to rules. People no longer deferred to the senior authority figure in the room; genuine dialogue neutralized hierarchical power in the battle over ideas. The tendency for each individual to promote his or her pet solution gave way to understanding other perspectives. A confidence in the ability of people in different units to work together and work things out emerged. The people with the most curious minds and interesting questions soon became the most respected.

As a result of confronting strategic and adaptive challenges, KPMG as a whole will move from auditing to assurance, from operations consulting to shaping corporate vision, from business-process reengineering to developing organizational capabilities, and from teaching traditional skills to its own clients to creating learning organizations. The task forces identified $50 million to $60 million worth of new business opportunities.

Many senior partners who had believed that a firm dominated by the auditing mentality could not contain creative people were surprised when the process unlocked creativity, passion, imagination, and a willingness to take risks. Two stories illustrate the fundamental changes that took place in the firm's mind-set.

We saw one middle manager develop the confidence to create a new business. He spotted the opportunity to provide KPMG services to virtual organizations and strategic alliances. He traveled the world, visiting the leaders of 65 virtual organizations. The results of his innovative research served as a resource to KPMG in entering this growing market. Moreover, he represented the new KPMG by giving a keynote address discussing his findings at a world forum. We also saw a 28-year-old female auditor skillfully guide a group of older, male senior partners through a complex day of looking at opportunities associated with implementing the firm's new strategies. That could not have occurred the year before. The senior partners never would have listened to such a voice from below.

Leadership as Learning

Many efforts to transform organizations through mergers and acquisitions, restructuring, reengineering, and strategy work falter because managers fail to grasp the requirements of adaptive work. They make the classic error of treating adaptive challenges like technical problems that can be solved by tough-minded senior executives.

The implications of that error go to the heart of the work of leaders in organizations today. Leaders crafting strategy have access to the technical expertise and the tools they need to calculate the benefits of a merger or restructuring, understand future trends and discontinuities, identify opportunities, map existing competencies, and identify the steering mechanisms to support their strategic direction. These tools and techniques are readily available both within organizations and from a variety of consulting firms, and they are very useful. In many cases, however, seemingly good strategies fail to be implemented. And often the failure is misdiagnosed: "We had a good strategy, but we couldn't execute it effectively."

In fact, the strategy itself is often deficient because too many perspectives were ignored during its formulation. The failure to do the necessary adaptive work during the strategy development process is a symptom of senior managers' technical orientation. Managers frequently derive their solution to a problem and then try to sell it to some colleagues and bypass or sandbag others in the commitment-building process. Too often, leaders, their team, and consultants fail to identify and tackle the adaptive dimensions of the challenge and to ask themselves, Who needs to learn what in order to develop, understand, commit to, and implement the strategy?

The same technical orientation entraps business-process-reengineering and restructuring initiatives, in which consultants and managers have the know-how to do the technical work of framing the objectives, designing a new work flow, documenting and communicating results, and identifying the activities to be performed by people in the organization. In many instances, reengineering falls short of the mark because it treats process redesign as a technical problem: Managers neglect to identify the adaptive work and involve the people who have to do the changing. Senior executives fail to invest their time and their souls in understanding these issues and guiding people through the transition. Indeed, engineering is itself the wrong metaphor.

In short, the prevailing notion that leadership consists of having a vision and aligning people with that vision is bankrupt because it continues to treat adaptive situations as if they were technical: The authority figure is supposed to divine where the company is going, and people are supposed to follow. Leadership is reduced to a combination of grand knowing and salesmanship. Such a perspective reveals a basic misconception about the way businesses succeed in addressing adaptive challenges. Adaptive situations are hard to define and resolve precisely because they demand the work and responsibility of managers and people throughout the organization. They are not amenable to solutions provided by leaders; adaptive solutions require members of the organization to take responsibility for the problematic situations that face them.

Leadership has to take place every day. It cannot be the responsibility of the few, a rare event, or a once-in-a-lifetime opportunity. In our world, in our businesses, we face adaptive challenges all the time. When an executive is asked to square conflicting aspirations, he and his people face an adaptive challenge. When a manager sees a solution to a problem—technical in many respects except that it requires a change in the attitudes and habits of subordinates—he faces an adaptive challenge. When an employee close to the front line sees a gap between the organization's purpose and the objectives he is asked to achieve, he faces both an adaptive challenge and the risks and opportunity of leading from below.

Leadership, as seen in this light, requires a learning strategy. A leader, from above or below, with or without authority, has to engage people in confronting the challenge, adjusting their values, changing perspectives, and learning new habits. To an authoritative person who prides himself on his ability to tackle hard problems, this shift may come as a rude awakening. But it also should ease the burden of having to know all the answers and bear all the load. To the person who waits to receive either the coach's call or "the vision" to lead, this change may also seem a mixture of good news and bad news. The adaptive demands of our time require leaders who take responsibility without waiting for revelation or request. One can lead with no more than a question in hand.

Originally published in January 1997. Reprint R0111K

Why Should Anyone Be Led by You?

by Robert Goffee and Gareth Jones

IF YOU WANT TO SILENCE a room of executives, try this small trick. Ask them, "Why would anyone want to be led by you?" We've asked just that question for the past ten years while consulting for dozens of companies in Europe and the United States. Without fail, the response is a sudden, stunned hush. All you can hear are knees knocking.

Executives have good reason to be scared. You can't do anything in business without followers, and followers in these "empowered" times are hard to find. So executives had better know what it takes to lead effectively—they must find ways to engage people and rouse their commitment to company goals. But most don't know how, and who can blame them? There's simply too much advice out there. Last year alone, more than 2,000 books on leadership were published, some of them even repackaging Moses and Shakespeare as leadership gurus.

We've yet to hear advice that tells the whole truth about leadership. Yes, everyone agrees that leaders need vision, energy, authority, and strategic direction. That goes without saying. But we've discovered that inspirational leaders also share four unexpected qualities:

- **They selectively show their weaknesses.** By exposing some vulnerability, they reveal their approachability and humanity.

- **They rely heavily on intuition to gauge the appropriate timing and course of their actions.** Their ability to collect and interpret soft data helps them know just when and how to act.

- **They manage employees with something we call tough empathy.** Inspirational leaders empathize passionately—and realistically—with people, and they care intensely about the work employees do.

- **They reveal their differences.** They capitalize on what's unique about themselves. You may find yourself in a top position without these qualities, but few people will want to be led by you.

Our theory about the four essential qualities of leadership, it should be noted, is not about results per se. While many of the leaders we have studied and use as examples do in fact post superior financial returns, the focus of our research has been on leaders who excel at inspiring people—in capturing hearts, minds, and souls. This ability is not everything in business, but any experienced leader will tell you it is worth quite a lot. Indeed, great results may be impossible without it.

Our research into leadership began some 25 years ago and has followed three streams since then. First, as academics, we ransacked the prominent leadership theories of the past century to develop our own working model of effective leadership. (For more on the history of leadership thinking, see the sidebar "Leadership: A Small History of a Big Topic.") Second, as consultants, we have tested our theory with thousands of executives in workshops worldwide and through observations with dozens of clients. And third, as executives ourselves, we have vetted our theories in our own organizations.

Reveal Your Weaknesses

When leaders reveal their weaknesses, they show us who they are—warts and all. This may mean admitting that they're irritable on Monday mornings, that they are somewhat disorganized, or even

Idea in Brief

The question "Why should anyone be led by you?" strikes fear in the hearts of most executives. With good reason. You can't get anything done without followers, and in these "empowered" times, followers are hard to find—*except* by leaders who excel at capturing people's hearts, minds, and spirits.

How do you do that? Of course, you need vision, energy, authority, and strategic direction—*and* these four additional qualities:

- Show you're human, selectively revealing weaknesses.

- Be a "sensor," collecting soft people data that lets you rely on intuition.

- Manage employees with "tough empathy." Care passionately about them and their work, while giving them only what they *need* to achieve their best.

- Dare to be different, capitalizing on your uniqueness.

Mix and match these qualities to find the right style for the right moment.

Without all four qualities, you might climb to the top. But few people will want to follow you, and your company won't achieve its best results.

rather shy. Such admissions work because people need to see leaders own up to some flaw before they participate willingly in an endeavor. Exposing a weakness establishes trust and thus helps get folks on board. Indeed, if executives try to communicate that they're perfect at everything, there will be no need for anyone to help them with anything. They won't need followers. They'll signal that they can do it all themselves.

Beyond creating trust and a collaborative atmosphere, communicating a weakness also builds solidarity between followers and leaders. Consider a senior executive we know at a global management consultancy. He agreed to give a major presentation despite being badly afflicted by physical shaking caused by a medical condition. The otherwise highly critical audience greeted this courageous display of weakness with a standing ovation. By giving the talk, he had dared to say, "I am just like you—imperfect." Sharing an

Idea in Practice

Reveal Your Weaknesses

Nobody wants to work with a perfect leader—he doesn't appear to need help. So show you're human—warts and all. You'll build collaboration and solidarity between you and your followers, and underscore your approachability.

Tips:

- Don't expose a weakness that others see as fatal. (A new finance director shouldn't reveal his ignorance of discounted cash flow!) Choose a tangential weakness instead.

- Pick a flaw that others consider a strength, e.g., workaholism.

Become a Sensor

Hone your ability to collect and interpret subtle interpersonal cues, detecting what's going on without others' spelling it out.

Example: Franz Humer, highly successful CEO of Roche, a health-care research company, senses underlying currents of opinion, gauges unexpressed feelings, and accurately judges relationships' quality.

Tip:

- Test your perceptions: Validate them with a trusted advisor or inner-team member.

Practice Tough Empathy

Real leaders empathize fiercely with their followers and care

intensely about their people's work. They're also empathetically "tough." This means giving people not necessarily what they *want*, but what they *need* to achieve their best.

Example: BBC CEO Greg Dyke knew that to survive in a digital world, the company had to spend more on programs and less on people. He restructured the organization, but only after explaining this openly and directly to the staff. Though many employees lost jobs, Dyke kept people's commitment.

Dare to Be Different

Capitalizing on what's unique about yourself lets you signal your separateness as a leader, and motivates others to perform better. Followers push themselves more if their leader is just a little aloof.

Tips:

- Don't *over*differentiate yourself—you could lose contact with followers. Robert Horton, former CEO of British Petroleum, conspicuously displayed his formidable intelligence. Followers saw him as arrogant, and detached themselves from him. He was dismissed after three years.

- Distinguish yourself through qualities like imagination, expertise, and adventuresomeness.

imperfection is so effective because it underscores a human being's authenticity. Richard Branson, the founder of Virgin, is a brilliant businessman and a hero in the United Kingdom. (Indeed, the Virgin brand is so linked to him personally that succession is a significant issue.) Branson is particularly effective at communicating his vulnerability. He is ill at ease and fumbles incessantly when interviewed in public. It's a weakness, but it's Richard Branson. That's what revealing a weakness is all about: showing your followers that you are genuine and approachable—human and humane.

Another advantage to exposing a weakness is that it offers a leader valuable protection. Human nature being what it is, if you don't show some weakness, then observers may invent one for you. Celebrities and politicians have always known this. Often, they deliberately give the public something to talk about, knowing full well that if they don't, the newspapers will invent something even worse. Princess Diana may have aired her eating disorder in public, but she died with her reputation intact, indeed even enhanced.

That said, the most effective leaders know that exposing a weakness must be done carefully. They own up to *selective* weaknesses. Knowing which weakness to disclose is a highly honed art. The golden rule is never to expose a weakness that will be seen as a fatal flaw—by which we mean a flaw that jeopardizes central aspects of your professional role. Consider the new finance director of a major corporation. He can't suddenly confess that he's never understood discounted cash flow. A leader should reveal only a tangential flaw— and perhaps even several of them. Paradoxically, this admission will help divert attention away from major weaknesses.

Another well-known strategy is to pick a weakness that can in some ways be considered a strength, such as being a workaholic. When leaders expose these limited flaws, people won't see much of anything and little harm will come to them. There is an important caveat, however: if the leader's vulnerability is not perceived to be genuine, he won't gain anyone's support. Instead he will open himself up to derision and scorn. One scenario we saw repeatedly in our research was one in which a CEO feigns absentmindedness to conceal his

Leadership: A Small History of a Big Topic

PEOPLE HAVE BEEN TALKING about leadership since the time of Plato. But in organizations all over the world—in dinosaur conglomerates and new-economy startups alike—the same complaint emerges: we don't have enough leadership. We have to ask ourselves, Why are we so obsessed with leadership?

One answer is that there is a crisis of belief in the modern world that has its roots in the rationalist revolution of the eighteenth century. During the Enlightenment, philosophers such as Voltaire claimed that through the application of reason alone, people could control their destiny. This marked an incredibly optimistic turn in world history. In the nineteenth century, two beliefs stemmed from this rationalist notion: a belief in progress and a belief in the perfectibility of man. This produced an even rosier world view than before. It wasn't until the end of the nineteenth century, with the writings first of Sigmund Freud and later of Max Weber, that the chinks in the armor appeared. These two thinkers destroyed Western man's belief in rationality and progress. The current quest for leadership is a direct consequence of their work.

The founder of psychoanalysis, Freud theorized that beneath the surface of the rational mind was the unconscious. He supposed that the unconscious was responsible for a fair proportion of human behavior. Weber, the leading critic of Marx and a brilliant sociologist, also explored the limits of reason. Indeed, for him, the most destructive force operating in institutions was something he called technical rationality—that is, rationality without morality.

For Weber, technical rationality was embodied in one particular organizational form—the bureaucracy. Bureaucracies, he said, were frightening not for their inefficiencies but for their efficiencies and their capacity to dehumanize people. The tragic novels of Franz Kafka bear stark testimony to the

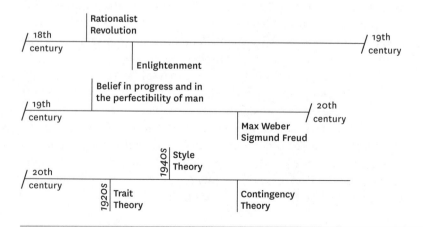

debilitating effects of bureaucracy. Even more chilling was the testimony of Hitler's lieutenant Adolf Eichmann that "I was just a good bureaucrat." Weber believed that the only power that could resist bureaucratization was charismatic leadership. But even this has a very mixed record in the twentieth century. Although there have been inspirational and transformational wartime leaders, there have also been charismatic leaders like Hitler, Stalin, and Mao Tse-tung who committed horrendous atrocities.

By the twentieth century, there was much skepticism about the power of reason and man's ability to progress continuously. Thus, for both pragmatic and philosophic reasons, an intense interest in the concept of leadership began to develop. And indeed, in the 1920s, the first serious research started. The first leadership theory—trait theory—attempted to identify the common characteristics of effective leaders. To that end, leaders were weighed and measured and subjected to a battery of psychological tests. But no one could identify what effective leaders had in common. Trait theory fell into disfavor soon after expensive studies concluded that effective leaders were either above-average height or below.

Trait theory was replaced by style theory in the 1940s, primarily in the United States. One particular style of leadership was singled out as having the most potential. It was a hail-fellow-well-met democratic style of leadership, and thousands of American executives were sent to training courses to learn how to behave this way. There was only one drawback. The theory was essentially capturing the spirit of FDR's America—open, democratic, and meritocratic. And so when McCarthyism and the Cold War surpassed the New Deal, a completely new style was required. Suddenly, everyone was encouraged to behave like a Cold War warrior! The poor executive was completely confused.

Recent leadership thinking is dominated by contingency theory, which says that leadership is dependent on a particular situation. That's fundamentally true, but given that there are endless contingencies in life, there are endless varieties of leadership. Once again, the beleaguered executive looking for a model to help him is hopelessly lost.

For this article, we ransacked all the leadership theories to come up with the four essential leadership qualities. Like Weber, we look at leadership that is primarily antibureaucratic and charismatic. From trait theory, we derived the qualities of weaknesses and differences. Unlike the original trait theorists, however, we do not believe that all leaders have the same weaknesses; our research only showed that all leaders expose some flaws. Tough empathy grew out of style theory, which looked at different kinds of relationships between leaders and their followers. Finally, context theory set the stage for needing to know what skills to use in various circumstances.

inconsistency or even dishonesty. This is a sure way to alienate follow-ers who will remember accurately what happened or what was said.

Become a Sensor

Inspirational leaders rely heavily on their instincts to know when to reveal a weakness or a difference. We call them good situation sen-sors, and by that we mean that they can collect and interpret soft data. They can sniff out the signals in the environment and sense what's going on without having anything spelled out for them.

Franz Humer, the CEO of Roche, is a classic sensor. He is highly accomplished in detecting shifts in climate and ambience; he can read subtle cues and sense underlying currents of opinion that elude less perceptive people. Humer says he developed this skill as a tour guide in his mid-twenties when he was responsible for groups of 100 or more. "There was no salary, only tips," he explains. "Pretty soon, I knew how to hone in on particular groups. Eventually, I could pre-dict within 10% how much I could earn from any particular group." Indeed, great sensors can easily gauge unexpressed feelings; they can very accurately judge whether relationships are working or not. The process is complex, and as anyone who has ever encountered it knows, the results are impressive.

Consider a human resources executive we worked with in a multinational entertainment company. One day he got news of a dis-tribution problem in Italy that had the potential to affect the com-pany's worldwide operations. As he was thinking about how to hide the information temporarily from the Paris-based CEO while he worked on a solution, the phone rang. It was the CEO saying, "Tell me, Roberto, what the hell's going on in Milan?" The CEO was al-ready aware that something was wrong. How? He had his networks, of course. But in large part, he was gifted at detecting information that wasn't aimed at him. He could read the silences and pick up on nonverbal cues in the organization.

Not surprisingly, the most impressive business leaders we have worked with are all very refined sensors. Ray van Schaik, the chair-man of Heineken in the early 1990s, is a good example. Conservative and urbane, van Schaik's genius lay in his ability to read signals he received from colleagues and from Freddie Heineken, the third-generation family member who was "always there without being there." While some senior managers spent a lot of time second-guessing the major shareholder, van Schaik developed an ability to "just know" what Heineken wanted. This ability was based on many years of working with him on the Heineken board, but it was more than that—van Schaik could read Heineken even though they had very different personalities and didn't work together directly.

Success stories like van Schaik's come with a word of warning. While leaders must be great sensors, sensing can create problems. That's because in making fine judgments about how far they can go, leaders risk losing their followers. The political situation in Northern Ireland is a powerful example. Over the past two years, several leaders—David Trimble, Gerry Adams, and Tony Blair, together with George Mitchell—have taken unprecedented initiatives toward peace. At every step of the way, these leaders had to sense how far they could go without losing their electorates. In business, think of mergers and acquisitions. Unless organizational leaders and negotiators can convince their followers in a timely way that the move is positive, value and goodwill quickly erode. This is the situation recently faced by Vodafone and France Telecom in the sale and purchase of Orange.

There is another danger associated with sensing skills. By definition, sensing a situation involves projection—that state of mind whereby you attribute your own ideas to other people and things. When a person "projects," his thoughts may interfere with the truth. Imagine a radio that picks up any number of signals, many of which are weak and distorted. Situation sensing is like that; you can't always be sure what you're hearing because of all the static. The employee who sees her boss distracted and leaps to the conclusion that she is going to be fired is a classic example. Most skills become heightened under threat, but particularly during situation sensing. Such oversensitivity in a leader can be a recipe for disaster. For this reason, sensing capability must always be framed by reality testing. Even the most gifted sensor may need to validate his perceptions with a trusted adviser or a member of his inner team.

Practice Tough Empathy

Unfortunately, there's altogether too much hype nowadays about the idea that leaders *must* show concern for their teams. There's nothing worse than seeing a manager return from the latest interpersonal-skills training program with "concern" for others. Real leaders don't need a training program to convince their employees that they care. Real leaders empathize fiercely with the people they lead. They also care intensely about the work their employees do.

Consider Alain Levy, the former CEO of Polygram. Although he often comes across as a rather aloof intellectual, Levy is well able to close the distance between himself and his followers. On one occasion, he helped some junior record executives in Australia choose singles off albums. Picking singles is a critical task in the music business: the selection of a song can make or break the album. Levy sat down with the young people and took on the work with passion. "You bloody idiots," he added his voice to the melee, "you don't know what the hell you're talking about; we always have a dance track first!" Within 24 hours, the story spread throughout the company; it was the best PR Levy ever got. "Levy really knows how to pick singles," people said. In fact, he knew how to identify with the work, and he knew how to enter his followers' world—one where strong, colorful language is the norm—to show them that he cared.

Clearly, as the above example illustrates, we do not believe that the empathy of inspirational leaders is the soft kind described in so much of the management literature. On the contrary, we feel that real leaders manage through a unique approach we call tough empathy. Tough empathy means giving people what they need, not what they want. Organizations like the Marine Corps and consulting firms specialize in tough empathy. Recruits are pushed to be the best that they can be; "grow or go" is the motto. Chris Satterwaite, the CEO of ell Pottinger Communications and a former chief executive of several ad agencies, understands what tough empathy is all about. He adeptly handles the challenges of managing creative people while making tough decisions. "If I have to, I can be ruthless," he says. "But while they're with me, I promise my people that they'll learn."

Four Popular Myths About Leadership

IN BOTH OUR RESEARCH AND consulting work, we have seen executives who profoundly misunderstand what makes an inspirational leader. Here are four of the most common myths:

Everyone can be a leader.

Not true. Many executives don't have the self-knowledge or the authenticity necessary for leadership. And self-knowledge and authenticity are only part of the equation. Individuals must also want to be leaders, and many talented employees are not interested in shouldering that responsibility. Others prefer to devote more time to their private lives than to their work. After all, there is more to life than work, and more to work than being the boss.

Leaders deliver business results.

Not always. If results were always a matter of good leadership, picking leaders would be easy. In every case, the best strategy would be to go after people in companies with the best results. But clearly, things are not that simple. Businesses in quasi-monopolistic industries can often do very well with competent management rather than great leadership. Equally, some well-led businesses do not necessarily produce results, particularly in the short term.

People who get to the top are leaders.

Not necessarily. One of the most persistent misperceptions is that people in leadership positions are leaders. But people who make it to the top may have done so because of political acumen, not necessarily because of true leadership quality. What's more, real leaders are found all over the organization, from the executive suite to the shop floor. By definition, leaders are simply people who have followers, and rank doesn't have much to do with that. Effective military organizations like the U.S. Navy have long realized the importance of developing leaders throughout the organization.

Leaders are great coaches.

Rarely. A whole cottage industry has grown up around the teaching that good leaders ought to be good coaches. But that thinking assumes that a single person can both inspire the troops and impart technical skills. Of course, it's possible that great leaders may also be great coaches, but we see that only occasionally. More typical are leaders like Steve Jobs whose distinctive strengths lie in their ability to excite others through their vision rather than through their coaching talents.

At its best, tough empathy balances respect for the individual and for the task at hand. Attending to both, however, isn't easy, especially when the business is in survival mode. At such times, caring leaders have to give selflessly to the people around them and know when to pull back. Consider a situation at Unilever at a time when it was developing Persil Power, a detergent that eventually had to be removed from the market because it destroyed clothes that were laundered in it. Even though the product was showing early signs of trouble, CEO Niall FitzGerald stood by his troops. "That was the popular place to be, but I should not have been there," he says now. "I should have stood back, cool and detached, looked at the whole field, watched out for the customer." But caring with detachment is not easy, especially since, when done right, tough empathy is harder on you than on your employees. "Some theories of leadership make caring look effortless. It isn't," says Paulanne Mancuso, president and CEO of Calvin Klein Cosmetics. "You have to do things you don't want to do, and that's hard." It's tough to be tough.

Tough empathy also has the benefit of impelling leaders to take risks. When Greg Dyke took over at the BBC, his commercial competitors were able to spend substantially more on programs than the BBC could. Dyke quickly realized that in order to thrive in a digital world, the BBC needed to increase its expenditures. He explained this openly and directly to the staff. Once he had secured their buy-in, he began thoroughly restructuring the organization. Although many employees were let go, he was able to maintain people's commitment. Dyke attributed his success to his tough empathy with employees: "Once you have the people with you, you can make the difficult decisions that need to be made."

One final point about tough empathy: those more apt to use it are people who really care about something. And when people care deeply about something—anything—they're more likely to show their true selves. They will not only communicate authenticity, which is the precondition for leadership, but they will show that they are doing more than just playing a role. People do not commit to executives who merely live up to the obligations of their jobs.

Can Female Leaders Be True to Themselves?

GENDER DIFFERENCES CAN BE used to either positive or negative effect. Women, in particular, are prone to being stereotyped according to differences—albeit usually not the ones that they would choose. Partly this is because there are fewer women than men in management positions. According to research in social psychology, if a group's representation falls below 20% in a given society, then it's going to be subjected to stereotyping whether it likes it or not. For women, this may mean being typecast as a "helper," "nurturer," or "seductress"—labels that may prevent them from defining their own differences.

In earlier research, we discovered that many women—particularly women in their fifties—try to avoid this dynamic by disappearing. They try to make themselves invisible. They wear clothes that disguise their bodies; they try to blend in with men by talking tough. That's certainly one way to avoid negative stereotyping, but the problem is that it reduces a woman's chances of being seen as a potential leader. She's not promoting her real self and differences.

Another response to negative stereotyping is to collectively resist it—for example, by mounting a campaign that promotes the rights, opportunities, and even the number of women in the workplace. But on a day-to-day basis, survival is often all women have time for, therefore making it impossible for them to organize themselves formally.

A third response that emerged in our research was that women play into stereotyping to personal advantage. Some women, for example, knowingly play the role of "nurturer" at work, but they do it with such wit and skill that they are able to benefit from it. The cost of such a strategy?

It furthers harmful stereotypes and continues to limit opportunities for other women to communicate their genuine personal differences.

They want more. They want someone who cares passionately about the people and the work—just as they do.

Dare to Be Different

Another quality of inspirational leaders is that they capitalize on what's unique about themselves. In fact, using these differences to great advantage is the most important quality of the four we've mentioned. The most effective leaders deliberately use differences to keep a social distance. Even as they are drawing their followers close to them, inspirational leaders signal their separateness.

Often, a leader will show his differences by having a distinctly different dress style or physical appearance, but typically he will move on to distinguish himself through qualities like imagination, loyalty, expertise, or even a handshake. Anything can be a difference, but it is important to communicate it. Most people, however, are hesitant to communicate what's unique about themselves, and it can take years for them to be fully aware of what sets them apart. This is a serious disadvantage in a world where networking is so critical and where teams need to be formed overnight.

Some leaders know exactly how to take advantage of their differences. Take Sir John Harvey-Jones, the former CEO of ICI—what was once the largest manufacturing company in the United Kingdom. When he wrote his autobiography a few years ago, a British newspaper advertised the book with a sketch of Harvey-Jones. The profile had a moustache, long hair, and a loud tie. The drawing was in black and white, but everyone knew who it was. Of course, John Harvey-Jones didn't get to the top of ICI because of eye-catching ties and long hair. But he was very clever in developing differences that he exploited to show that he was adventurous, entrepreneurial, and unique—he was John Harvey-Jones.

There are other people who aren't as aware of their differences but still use them to great effect. For instance, Richard Surface, former managing director of the UK-based Pearl Insurance, always walked the floor and overtook people, using his own pace as a means of communicating urgency. Still other leaders are fortunate enough to have colleagues point out their differences for them. As the BBC's Greg Dyke puts it, "My partner tells me, 'You do things instinctively that you don't understand. What I worry about is that in the process of understanding them you could lose them!'" Indeed, what emerged in our interviews is that most leaders start off not knowing what their differences are but eventually come to know—and use—them more effectively over time. Franz Humer at Roche, for instance, now realizes that he uses his emotions to evoke reactions in others.

Most of the differences we've described are those that tend to be apparent, either to the leader himself or to the colleagues around him. But there are differences that are more subtle but still have very powerful effects. For instance, David Prosser, the CEO of Legal and General, one of Europe's largest and most successful insurance companies, is an outsider. He is not a smooth city type; in fact, he comes from industrial South Wales. And though generally approachable, Prosser has a hard edge, which he uses in an understated but highly effective way. At a recent cocktail party, a rather excitable sales manager had been claiming how good the company was at cross-selling products. In a low voice, Prosser intervened: "We may be good, but we're not good enough." A chill swept through the room. What was Prosser's point? Don't feel so close you can relax! I'm the leader, and I make that call. Don't you forget it. He even uses this edge to good effect with the top team—it keeps everyone on their toes.

Inspirational leaders use separateness to motivate others to perform better. It is not that they are being Machiavellian but that they recognize instinctively that followers will push themselves if their leader is just a little aloof. Leadership, after all, is not a popularity contest.

One danger, of course, is that executives can overdifferentiate themselves in their determination to express their separateness. Indeed, some leaders lose contact with their followers, and doing so is fatal. Once they create too much distance, they stop being good sensors, and they lose the ability to identify and care. That's what appeared to happen during Robert Horton's tenure as chairman and CEO of BP during the early 1990s. Horton's conspicuous display of his considerable—indeed, daunting—intelligence sometimes led others to see him as arrogant and self-aggrandizing. That resulted in overdifferentiation, and it eventually contributed to Horton's dismissal just three years after he was appointed to the position.

Leadership in Action

All four of the qualities described here are necessary for inspirational leadership, but they cannot be used mechanically. They must become or must already be part of an executive's personality. That's why the "recipe" business books—those that prescribe to the Lee Iaccoca or Bill Gates way—often fail. No one can just ape another leader. So the challenge facing prospective leaders is for them to be themselves, but with more skill. That can be done by making yourself increasingly aware of the four leadership qualities we describe and by manipulating these qualities to come up with a personal style that works for you. Remember, there is no universal formula, and what's needed will vary from context to context. What's more, the results are often subtle, as the following story about Sir Richard Sykes, the highly successful chairman and CEO of Glaxo Wellcome, one of the world's leading pharmaceutical companies, illustrates.

When he was running the R&D division at Glaxo, Sykes gave a year-end review to the company's top scientists. At the end of the presentation, a researcher asked him about one of the company's new compounds, and the two men engaged in a short heated debate. The question-answer session continued for another 20 minutes, at the end of which the researcher broached the subject again. "Dr. Sykes," he began in a loud voice, "you have still failed to understand the structure of the new compound." You could feel Sykes's temper rise through the soles of his feet. He marched to the back of the room and displayed his anger before the intellectual brainpower of the entire company. "All right, lad," he yelled, "let us have a look at your notes!"

The Sykes story provides the ideal framework for discussing the four leadership qualities. To some people, Sykes's irritability could have seemed like inappropriate weakness. But in this context, his show of temper demonstrated Sykes's deep belief in the discussion about basic science—a company value. Therefore, his willingness to get angry actually cemented his credibility as a leader. He also showed that he was a very good sensor. If Sykes had exploded earlier in the meeting, he would have quashed the debate. Instead, his anger was perceived as defending the faith. The story also reveals

Sykes's ability to identify with his colleagues and their work. By talking to the researcher as a fellow scientist, he was able to create an empathic bond with his audience. He really cared, though his caring was clearly tough empathy. Finally, the story indicates Sykes's own willingness to show his differences. Despite being one of the United Kingdom's most successful businessmen, he has not conformed to "standard" English. On the contrary, Sykes proudly retains his distinctive northern accent. He also doesn't show the typical British reserve and decorum; he radiates passion. Like other real leaders, he acts and communicates naturally. Indeed, if we were to sum up the entire year-end review at Glaxo Wellcome, we'd say that Sykes was being himself—with great skill.

Unraveling the Mystery

As long as business is around, we will continue to pick apart the underlying ingredients of true leadership. And there will always be as many theories as there are questions. But of all the facets of leadership that one might investigate, there are few so difficult as understanding what it takes to develop leaders. The four leadership qualities are a necessary first step. Taken together, they tell executives to be authentic. As we counsel the executives we coach: "Be yourselves—more—with skill." There can be no advice more difficult to follow than that.

Originally published in September 2000. Reprint R00506

Crucibles
of Leadership

by Warren G. Bennis and Robert J. Thomas

AS LIFELONG STUDENTS OF LEADERSHIP, we are fascinated with the notion of what makes a leader. Why is it that certain people seem to naturally inspire confidence, loyalty, and hard work, while others (who may have just as much vision and smarts) stumble, again and again? It's a timeless question, and there's no simple answer. But we have come to believe it has something to do with the different ways that people deal with adversity. Indeed, our recent research has led us to conclude that one of the most reliable indicators and predictors of true leadership is an individual's ability to find meaning in negative events and to learn from even the most trying circumstances. Put another way, the skills required to conquer adversity and emerge stronger and more committed than ever are the same ones that make for extraordinary leaders.

Take Sidney Harman. Thirty-four years ago, the then-48-year-old businessman was holding down two executive positions. He was the chief executive of Harman Kardon (now Harman International), the audio components company he had cofounded, and he was serving as president of Friends World College, now Friends World Program, an experimental Quaker school on Long Island whose essential philosophy is that students, not their teachers, are responsible for their education. Juggling the two jobs, Harman was living what he calls a "bifurcated life," changing clothes in his car and eating lunch as he drove between Harman Kardon offices and plants and the Friends World campus. One day while at the college, he was told his company's factory in Bolivar, Tennessee, was having a crisis.

He immediately rushed to the Bolivar factory, a facility that was, as Harman now recalls, "raw, ugly, and, in many ways, demeaning." The problem, he found, had erupted in the polish and buff department, where a crew of a dozen workers, mostly African-Americans, did the dull, hard work of polishing mirrors and other parts, often under unhealthy conditions. The men on the night shift were supposed to get a coffee break at 10 PM. When the buzzer that announced the workers' break went on the fritz, management arbitrarily decided to postpone the break for ten minutes, when another buzzer was scheduled to sound. But one worker, "an old black man with an almost biblical name, Noah B. Cross," had "an epiphany," as Harman describes it. "He said, literally, to his fellow workers, 'I don't work for no buzzer. The buzzer works for me. It's my job to tell me when it's ten o'clock. I got me a watch. I'm not waiting another ten minutes. I'm going on my coffee break.' And all 12 guys took their coffee break, and, of course, all hell broke loose."

The worker's principled rebellion—his refusal to be cowed by management's senseless rule—was, in turn, a revelation to Harman: "The technology is there to serve the men, not the reverse," he remembers realizing. "I suddenly had this awakening that everything I was doing at the college had appropriate applications in business." In the ensuing years, Harman revamped the factory and its workings, turning it into a kind of campus—offering classes on the premises, including piano lessons, and encouraging the workers to take most of the responsibility for running their workplace. Further, he created an environment where dissent was not only tolerated but also encouraged. The plant's lively independent newspaper, the *Bolivar Mirror,* gave workers a creative and emotional outlet—and they enthusiastically skewered Harman in its pages.

Harman had, unexpectedly, become a pioneer of participative management, a movement that continues to influence the shape of workplaces around the world. The concept wasn't a grand idea conceived in the CEO's office and imposed on the plant, Harman says. It

Idea in Brief

What enables one leader to inspire confidence, loyalty, and hard work, while others—with equal vision and intelligence—stumble? How individuals deal with adversity provides a clue.

Extraordinary leaders find meaning in—and learn from—the most negative events. Like phoenixes rising from the ashes, they emerge from adversity stronger, more confident in themselves and their purpose, and more committed to their work.

Such transformative events are called **crucibles**—a severe test or trial. Crucibles are intense, often traumatic—and always unplanned.

grew organically out of his going down to Bolivar to, in his words, "put out this fire." Harman's transformation was, above all, a creative one. He had connected two seemingly unrelated ideas and created a radically different approach to management that recognized both the economic and humane benefits of a more collegial workplace. Harman went on to accomplish far more during his career. In addition to founding Harman International, he served as the deputy secretary of commerce under Jimmy Carter. But he always looked back on the incident in Bolivar as the formative event in his professional life, the moment he came into his own as a leader.

The details of Harman's story are unique, but their significance is not. In interviewing more than 40 top leaders in business and the public sector over the past three years, we were surprised to find that all of them—young and old—were able to point to intense, often traumatic, always unplanned experiences that had transformed them and had become the sources of their distinctive leadership abilities.

We came to call the experiences that shape leaders "crucibles," after the vessels medieval alchemists used in their attempts to turn base metals into gold. For the leaders we interviewed, the crucible experience was a trial and a test, a point of deep self-reflection that forced them to question who they were and what mattered to them. It required them to examine their values, question their assumptions, hone their judgment. And, invariably, they emerged from the crucible stronger and more sure of themselves and their purpose—changed in some fundamental way.

Idea in Practice

The Crucible Experience

Crucibles force leaders into deep self-reflection, where they examine their values, question their assumptions, and hone their judgment.

Example: Sidney Harman—co-founder of audio components company Harman Kardon and president of an experimental college encouraging student-driven education—encountered his crucible when "all hell broke loose" in one of his factories. After managers postponed a scheduled break because the buzzer didn't sound, workers rebelled. "I don't work for no buzzer," one proclaimed.

To Harman, this refusal to bow to management's senseless rule suggested a surprising link between student-driven education and business. Pioneering participative management,

Harman transformed his plant into a kind of campus, offering classes and encouraging dissent. He considers the rebellion the formative event in his career—the moment he became a true leader.

The Many Shapes of Crucibles

Some crucibles are violent and life-threatening (encounters with prejudice, illness); others are more positive, yet profoundly challenging (such as demanding bosses or mentors). Whatever the shape, leaders create a narrative telling how they met the challenge and became better for it.

Example: While working for former Atlanta mayor Robert F. Maddox, Vernon Jordan endured repeated racial heckling from Maddox. Rather than letting Maddox's sadism destroy him, Jordan interpreted the behavior as a desperate lashing out by someone who

Leadership crucibles can take many forms. Some are violent, life-threatening events. Others are more prosaic episodes of self-doubt. But whatever the crucible's nature, the people we spoke with were able, like Harman, to create a narrative around it, a story of how they were challenged, met the challenge, and became better leaders. As we studied these stories, we found that they not only told us how individual leaders are shaped but also pointed to some characteristics that seem common to all leaders—characteristics that were formed, or at least exposed, in the crucible.

knew the era of the Old South was ending. Jordan's response empowered him to become an esteemed lawyer and presidential advisor.

Essential Leadership Skills

Four skills enable leaders to learn from adversity:

1. **Engage others in shared meaning.** For example, Sidney Harman mobilized employees around a radical new management approach—amid a factory crisis.

2. **A distinctive, compelling voice.** With words alone, college president Jack Coleman preempted a violent clash between the football team and anti-Vietnam War demonstrators threatening to burn the American flag. Coleman's suggestion to the protestors? Lower the flag, wash it, then put it back up.

3. **Integrity.** Coleman's values prevailed during the emotionally charged face-off between antiwar demonstrators and irate football players.

4. **Adaptive capacity.** This most critical skill includes the *ability to grasp context,* and *hardiness.* Grasping context requires weighing many factors (e.g., how different people will interpret a gesture). Without this quality, leaders can't connect with constituents.

Hardiness provides the perseverance and toughness needed to remain hopeful despite disaster. For instance, Michael Klein made millions in real estate during his teens, lost it all by age 20—then built several more businesses, including transforming a tiny software company into a Hewlett-Packard acquisition.

Learning from Difference

A crucible is, by definition, a transformative experience through which an individual comes to a new or an altered sense of identity. It is perhaps not surprising then that one of the most common types of crucibles we documented involves the experience of prejudice. Being a victim of prejudice is particularly traumatic because it forces an individual to confront a distorted picture of him- or herself, and it often unleashes profound feelings of anger, bewilderment, and even withdrawal. For all its trauma, however, the experience of prejudice is for some a clarifying event. Through it, they gain a clearer vision of who they are, the role they play, and their place in the world.

Consider, for example, Liz Altman, now a Motorola vice president, who was transformed by the year she spent at a Sony camcorder factory in rural Japan, where she faced both estrangement and sexism. It was, says Altman, "by far, the hardest thing I've ever done." The foreign culture—particularly its emphasis on groups over individuals—was both a shock and a challenge to a young American woman. It wasn't just that she felt lonely in an alien world. She had to face the daunting prospect of carving out a place for herself as the only woman engineer in a plant, and nation, where women usually serve as low-level assistants and clerks known as "office ladies."

Another woman who had come to Japan under similar circumstances had warned Altman that the only way to win the men's respect was to avoid becoming allied with the office ladies. But on her very first morning, when the bell rang for a coffee break, the men headed in one direction and the women in another—and the women saved her a place at their table, while the men ignored her. Instinct told Altman to ignore the warning rather than insult the women by rebuffing their invitation.

Over the next few days, she continued to join the women during breaks, a choice that gave her a comfortable haven from which to observe the unfamiliar office culture. But it didn't take her long to notice that some of the men spent the break at their desks reading magazines, and Altman determined that she could do the same on occasion. Finally, after paying close attention to the conversations around her, she learned that several of the men were interested in mountain biking. Because Altman wanted to buy a mountain bike, she approached them for advice. Thus, over time, she established herself as something of a free agent, sometimes sitting with the women and other times engaging with the men.

And as it happened, one of the women she'd sat with on her very first day, the department secretary, was married to one of the engineers. The secretary took it upon herself to include Altman in social gatherings, a turn of events that probably wouldn't have occurred if Altman had alienated her female coworkers on that first day. "Had I just gone to try to break in with [the men] and not had her as an ally, it would never have happened," she says.

Looking back, Altman believes the experience greatly helped her gain a clearer sense of her personal strengths and capabilities, preparing her for other difficult situations. Her tenure in Japan taught her to observe closely and to avoid jumping to conclusions based on cultural assumptions—invaluable skills in her current position at Motorola, where she leads efforts to smooth alliances with other corporate cultures, including those of Motorola's different regional operations.

Altman has come to believe that she wouldn't have been as able to do the Motorola job if she hadn't lived in a foreign country and experienced the dissonance of cultures: ". . . even if you're sitting in the same room, ostensibly agreeing . . . unless you understand the frame of reference, you're probably missing a bunch of what's going on." Altman also credits her crucible with building her confidence—she feels that she can cope with just about anything that comes her way.

People can feel the stigma of cultural differences much closer to home, as well. Muriel ("Mickie") Siebert, the first woman to own a seat on the New York Stock Exchange, found her crucible on the Wall Street of the 1950s and 1960s, an arena so sexist that she couldn't get a job as a stockbroker until she took her first name off her résumé and substituted a genderless initial. Other than the secretaries and the occasional analyst, women were few and far between. That she was Jewish was another strike against her at a time, she points out, when most of big business was "not nice" to either women or Jews. But Siebert wasn't broken or defeated. Instead, she emerged stronger, more focused, and more determined to change the status quo that excluded her.

When we interviewed Siebert, she described her way of addressing anti-Semitism—a technique that quieted the offensive comments of her peers without destroying the relationships she needed to do her job effectively. According to Siebert, at the time it was part of doing business to have a few drinks at lunch. She remembers, "Give somebody a couple of drinks, and they would talk about the Jews." She had a greeting card she used for those occasions that went like this:

Roses are reddish,
Violets are bluish,
In case you don't know,
I am Jewish.

Siebert would have the card hand-delivered to the person who had made the anti-Semitic remarks, and on the card she had written, "Enjoyed lunch." As she recounts, "They got that card in the afternoon, and I never had to take any of that nonsense again. And I never embarrassed anyone, either." It was because she was unable to get credit for the business she was bringing in at any of the large Wall Street firms that she bought a seat on the New York Stock Exchange and started working for herself.

In subsequent years, she went on to found Muriel Siebert & Company (now Siebert Financial Corporation) and has dedicated herself to helping other people avoid some of the difficulties she faced as a young professional. A prominent advocate for women in business and a leader in developing financial products directed at women, she's also devoted to educating children about financial opportunities and responsibility.

We didn't interview lawyer and presidential adviser Vernon Jordan for this article, but he, too, offers a powerful reminder of how prejudice can prove transformational rather than debilitating. In *Vernon Can Read! A Memoir* (Public Affairs, 2001), Jordan describes the vicious baiting he was subjected to as a young man. The man who treated him in this offensive way was his employer, Robert F. Maddox. Jordan served the racist former mayor of Atlanta at dinner, in a white jacket, with a napkin over his arm. He also functioned as Maddox's chauffeur. Whenever Maddox could, he would derisively announce, "Vernon can read!" as if the literacy of a young African-American were a source of wonderment.

Geeks and Geezers

WE DIDN'T SET OUT TO LEARN about crucibles. Our research for this article and for our new book, *Geeks and Geezers,* was actually designed to uncover the ways that *era* influences a leader's motivation and aspirations. We interviewed 43 of today's top leaders in business and the public sector, limiting our subjects to people born in or before 1925, or in or after 1970. To our delight, we learned a lot about how age and era affect leadership style.

Our geeks and geezers (the affectionate shorthand we eventually used to describe the two groups) had very different ideas about paying your dues, work-life balance, the role of heroes, and more. But they also shared some striking similarities—among them a love of learning and strong sense of values. Most intriguing, though, both our geeks and our geezers told us again and again how certain experiences inspired them, shaped them, and, indeed, taught them to lead. And so, as the best research often does, our work turned out to be even more interesting than we thought it would be. We continued to explore the influences of era—our findings are described in our book—but at the same time we probed for stories of these crucible experiences. These are the stories we share with you here.

Subjected to this type of abuse, a lesser man might have allowed Maddox to destroy him. But in his memoir, Jordan gives his own interpretation of Maddox's sadistic heckling, a tale that empowered Jordan instead of embittering him. When he looked at Maddox through the rearview mirror, Jordan did not see a powerful member of Georgia's ruling class. He saw a desperate anachronism, a person who lashed out because he knew his time was up. As Jordan writes about Maddox, "His half-mocking, half-serious comments about my education were the death rattle of his culture. When he saw that I was . . . crafting a life for myself that would make me a man in . . . ways he thought of as being a man, he was deeply unnerved."

Maddox's cruelty was the crucible that, consciously or not, Jordan imbued with redemptive meaning. Instead of lashing out or being paralyzed with hatred, Jordan saw the fall of the Old South and imagined his own future freed of the historical shackles of racism. His ability to organize meaning around a potential crisis turned it into the crucible around which his leadership was forged.

Reinvention in the Extreme:
The Power of Neoteny

ALL OF OUR INTERVIEW SUBJECTS described their crucibles as opportunities for reinvention—for taking stock of their lives and finding meaning in circumstances many people would see as daunting and potentially incapacitating. In the extreme, this capacity for reinvention comes to resemble eternal youth—a kind of vigor, openness, and an enduring capacity for wonder that is the antithesis of stereotyped old age.

We borrowed a term from biology—"neoteny," which, according to the *American Heritage Dictionary,* means "retention of juvenile characteristics in the adults of a species"—to describe this quality, this delight in lifelong learning, which every leader we interviewed displayed, regardless of age. To a person, they were full of energy, curiosity, and confidence that the world is a place of wonders spread before them like an endless feast.

Robert Galvin, former Motorola chairman now in his late 70s, spends his weekends windsurfing. Arthur Levitt, Jr., former SEC chairman who turned 71 this year, is an avid Outward Bound trekker. And architect Frank Gehry is now a 72-year-old ice hockey player. But it's not only an affinity for physical activity that characterizes neoteny—it's an appetite for learning and self-development, a curiosity and passion for life.

To understand why this quality is so powerful in a leader, it might help to take a quick look at the scientific principle behind it—neoteny as an evolutionary engine. It is the winning, puppyish quality of certain ancient wolves that allowed them to evolve into dogs. Over thousands of years, humans favored wolves that were the friendliest, most approachable, and most curious. Naturally, people were most drawn to the wolves least likely to attack without warning, that readily locked eyes with them, and that seemed almost human in their eager response to people; the ones, in short, that stayed the most like puppies. Like human infants, they have certain physical qualities that elicit a nurturing response in human adults.

Prevailing over Darkness

Some crucible experiences illuminate a hidden and suppressed area of the soul. These are often among the harshest of crucibles, involving, for instance, episodes of illness or violence. In the case of Sidney Rittenberg, now 79, the crucible took the form of 16 years of unjust imprisonment, in solitary confinement, in Communist China. In 1949

When infants see an adult, they often respond with a smile that begins small and slowly grows into a radiant grin that makes the adult feel at center of the universe. Recent studies of bonding indicate that nursing and other intimate interactions with an infant cause the mother's system to be flooded with oxytocin, a calming, feel-good hormone that is a powerful antidote to cortisol, the hormone produced by stress. Oxytocin appears to be the glue that produces bonding. And the baby's distinctive look and behaviors cause oxytocin to be released in the fortunate adult. That appearance—the one that pulls an involuntary "aaah" out of us whenever we see a baby—and those oxytocin-inducing behaviors allow infants to recruit adults to be their nurturers, essential if such vulnerable and incompletely developed creatures are to survive.

The power of neoteny to recruit protectors and nurturers was vividly illustrated in the former Soviet Union. Forty years ago, a Soviet scientist decided to start breeding silver foxes for neoteny at a Siberian fur farm. The goal was to create a tamer fox that would go with less fuss to slaughter than the typical silver fox. Only the least aggressive, most approachable animals were bred.

The experiment continued for 40 years, and today, after 35 generations, the farm is home to a breed of tame foxes that look and act more like juvenile foxes and even dogs than like their wild forebears. The physical changes in the animals are remarkable (some have floppy, dog-like ears), but what is truly stunning is the change neoteny has wrought in the human response to them. Instead of taking advantage of the fact that these neotenic animals don't snap and snarl on the way to their deaths, their human keepers appear to have been recruited by their newly cute and endearing charges. The keepers and the foxes appear to have formed close bonds, so close that the keepers are trying to find ways to save the animals from slaughter.

Rittenberg was initially jailed, without explanation, by former friends in Chairman Mao Zedong's government and spent his first year in total darkness when he wasn't being interrogated. (Rittenberg later learned that his arrest came at the behest of Communist Party officials in Moscow, who had wrongly identified him as a CIA agent.) Thrown into jail, confined to a tiny, pitch-dark cell, Rittenberg did not rail or panic. Instead, within minutes, he remembered a stanza of verse, four lines recited to him when he was a small child:

They drew a circle that shut me out,
Heretic, rebel, a thing to flout.
But love and I had the wit to win,
We drew a circle that took them in!

That bit of verse (adapted from "Outwitted," a poem by Edwin Markham) was the key to Rittenberg's survival. "My God," he thought, "there's my strategy." He drew the prison guards into his circle, developing relationships that would help him adapt to his confinement. Fluent in Chinese, he persuaded the guards to deliver him books and, eventually, provide a candle so that he could read. He also decided, after his first year, to devote himself to improving his mind—making it more scientific, more pure, and more dedicated to socialism. He believed that if he raised his consciousness, his captors would understand him better. And when, over time, the years in the dark began to take an intellectual toll on him and he found his reason faltering, he could still summon fairy tales and childhood stories such as *The Little Engine That Could* and take comfort from their simple messages.

By contrast, many of Rittenberg's fellow prisoners either lashed out in anger or withdrew. "They tended to go up the wall . . . They couldn't make it. And I think the reason was that they didn't understand . . . that happiness . . . is not a function of your circumstances; it's a function of your outlook on life."

Rittenberg's commitment to his ideals continued upon his release. His cell door opened suddenly in 1955, after his first six-year term in prison. He recounts, "Here was a representative of the central government telling me that I had been wronged, that the government was making a formal apology to me . . . and that they would do everything possible to make restitution." When his captors offered him money to start a new life in the United States or to travel in Europe, Rittenberg declined, choosing instead to stay in China and continue his work for the Communist Party.

And even after a second arrest, which put him into solitary confinement for ten years as retaliation for his support of open democracy during the Cultural Revolution, Rittenberg did not allow his spirit to be broken. Instead, he used his time in prison as an opportunity to question his belief system—in particular, his commitment to Marxism and Chairman Mao. "In that sense, prison emancipated me," he says.

Rittenberg studied, read, wrote, and thought, and he learned something about himself in the process: "I realized I had this great fear of being a turncoat, which . . . was so powerful that it prevented me from even looking at [my assumptions] . . . Even to question was an act of betrayal. After I got out . . . the scales fell away from my eyes and I understood that . . . the basic doctrine of arriving at democracy through dictatorship was wrong."

What's more, Rittenberg emerged from prison certain that absolutely nothing in his professional life could break him and went on to start a company with his wife. Rittenberg Associates is a consulting firm dedicated to developing business ties between the United States and China. Today, Rittenberg is as committed to his ideals—if not to his view of the best way to get there—as he was 50 years ago, when he was so severely tested.

Meeting Great Expectations

Fortunately, not all crucible experiences are traumatic. In fact, they can involve a positive, if deeply challenging, experience such as having a demanding boss or mentor. Judge Nathaniel R. Jones of the U.S. Court of Appeals for the Sixth Circuit, for instance, attributes much of his success to his interaction with a splendid mentor. That mentor was J. Maynard Dickerson, a successful attorney—the first black city prosecutor in the United States—and editor of a local African-American newspaper.

Dickerson influenced Jones at many levels. For instance, the older man brought Jones behind the scenes to witness firsthand the great civil rights struggle of the 1950s, inviting him to sit in on conversations with activists like Thurgood Marshall, Walter White, Roy

Wilkins, and Robert C. Weaver. Says Jones, "I was struck by their re-solve, their humor . . . and their determination not to let the system define them. Rather than just feel beaten down, they turned it around." The experience no doubt influenced the many important opinions Judge Jones has written in regard to civil rights.

Dickerson was both model and coach. His lessons covered every aspect of Jones's intellectual growth and presentation of self, includ-ing schooling in what we now call "emotional intelligence." Dicker-son set the highest standards for Jones, especially in the area of communication skills—a facility we've found essential to leader-ship. Dickerson edited Jones's early attempts at writing a sports col-umn with respectful ruthlessness, in red ink, as Jones remembers to this day—marking up the copy so that it looked, as Jones says, "like something chickens had a fight over." But Dickerson also took the time to explain every single mistake and why it mattered.

His mentor also expected the teenage Jones to speak correctly at all times and would hiss discreetly in his direction if he stumbled. Great expectations are evidence of great respect, and as Jones learned all the complex, often subtle lessons of how to succeed, he was motivated in no small measure by his desire not to disappoint the man he still calls "Mr. Dickerson." Dickerson gave Jones the kind of intensive mentoring that was tantamount to grooming him for a kind of professional and moral succession—and Jones has indeed become an instrument for the profound societal change for which Dickerson fought so courageously as well. Jones found life-changing meaning in the attention Dickerson paid to him—attention fueled by a conviction that he, too, though only a teenager, had a vital role to play in society and an important destiny.

Another story of a powerful mentor came to us from Michael Klein, a young man who made millions in Southern California real estate while still in his teens, only to lose it by the time he turned 20 and then go on to start several other businesses. His mentor was his grandfather Max S. Klein, who created the paint-by-numbers fad that swept the United States in the 1950s and 1960s. Klein was only four or five years old when his grandfather approached him and of-fered to share his business expertise. Over the years, Michael Klein's grandfather taught him to learn from and to cope with change, and the two spoke by phone for an hour every day until shortly before Max Klein's death.

The Essentials of Leadership

In our interviews, we heard many other stories of crucible experiences. Take Jack Coleman, 78-year-old former president of Haverford College in Pennsylvania. He told us of one day, during the Vietnam War, when he heard that a group of students was planning to pull down the American flag and burn it—and that former members of the school's football team were going to make sure the students didn't succeed. Seemingly out of nowhere, Coleman had the idea to preempt the violence by suggesting that the protesting students take down the flag, wash it, and then put it back up—a crucible moment that even now elicits tremendous emotion in Coleman as he describes that day.

There's also Common Cause founder John W. Gardner, who died earlier this year at 89. He identified his arduous training as a Marine during World War II as the crucible in which his leadership abilities emerged. Architect Frank Gehry spoke of the biases he experienced as a Jew in college. Jeff Wilke, a general manager at a major manufacturer, told us of the day he learned that an employee had been killed in his plant—an experience that taught him that leadership was about much more than making quarterly numbers.

So, what allowed these people to not only cope with these difficult situations but also learn from them? We believe that great leaders possess four essential skills, and, we were surprised to learn, these happen to be the same skills that allow a person to find meaning in what could be a debilitating experience. First is the ability to engage others in shared meaning. Consider Sidney Harman, who dived into a chaotic work environment to mobilize employees around an entirely new approach to management. Second is a distinctive and compelling voice. Look at Jack Coleman's ability to defuse a potentially violent situation with only his words. Third is a sense of integrity (including a strong set of values). Here, we point again to Coleman, whose values prevailed even during the emotionally charged clash between peace demonstrators and the angry (and strong) former football team members.

But by far the most critical skill of the four is what we call "adaptive capacity." This is, in essence, applied creativity—an almost magical ability to transcend adversity, with all its attendant stresses, and to emerge stronger than before. It's composed of two primary qualities: the ability to grasp context, and hardiness. The ability to grasp context implies an ability to weigh a welter of factors, ranging from how very different groups of people will interpret a gesture to being able to put a situation in perspective. Without this, leaders are utterly lost, because they cannot connect with their constituents. M. Douglas Ivester, who succeeded Roberto Goizueta at Coca-Cola, exhibited a woeful inability to grasp context, lasting just 28 months on the job. For example, he demoted his highest-ranked African-American employee even as the company was losing a $200 million class-action suit brought by black employees—and this in Atlanta, a city with a powerful African-American majority. Contrast Ivester with Vernon Jordan. Jordan realized his boss's time was up—not just his time in power, but the era that formed him. And so Jordan was able to see past the insults and recognize his boss's bitterness for what it was— desperate lashing out.

Hardiness is just what it sounds like—the perseverance and toughness that enable people to emerge from devastating circumstances without losing hope. Look at Michael Klein, who experienced failure but didn't let it defeat him. He found himself with a single asset—a tiny software company he'd acquired. Klein built it into Transoft Networks, which Hewlett-Packard acquired in 1999. Consider, too, Mickie Siebert, who used her sense of humor to curtail offensive conversations. Or Sidney Rittenberg's strength during his imprisonment. He drew on his personal memories and inner strength to emerge from his lengthy prison term without bitterness.

It is the combination of hardiness and ability to grasp context that, above all, allows a person to not only survive an ordeal, but to learn from it, and to emerge stronger, more engaged, and more committed than ever. These attributes allow leaders to grow from their crucibles, instead of being destroyed by them—to find opportunity where others might find only despair. This is the stuff of true leadership.

Originally published in September 2002. Reprint R0209B

Level 5 Leadership

The Triumph of Humility and
Fierce Resolve. *by Jim Collins*

IN 1971, A SEEMINGLY ordinary man named Darwin E. Smith was named chief executive of Kimberly-Clark, a stodgy old paper company whose stock had fallen 36% behind the general market during the previous 20 years. Smith, the company's mild-mannered in-house lawyer, wasn't so sure the board had made the right choice—a feeling that was reinforced when a Kimberly-Clark director pulled him aside and reminded him that he lacked some of the qualifications for the position. But CEO he was, and CEO he remained for 20 years.

What a 20 years it was. In that period, Smith created a stunning transformation at Kimberly-Clark, turning it into the leading consumer paper products company in the world. Under his stewardship, the company beat its rivals Scott Paper and Procter & Gamble. And in doing so, Kimberly-Clark generated cumulative stock returns that were 4.1 times greater than those of the general market, outperforming venerable companies such as Hewlett-Packard, 3M, Coca-Cola, and General Electric.

Smith's turnaround of Kimberly-Clark is one the best examples in the twentieth century of a leader taking a company from merely good to truly great. And yet few people—even ardent students of business history—have heard of Darwin Smith. He probably would have liked it that way. Smith is a classic example of a Level 5 leader—an individual who blends extreme personal humility with intense professional will. According to our five-year research study, executives who possess this paradoxical combination of traits are catalysts for the statistically rare event of transforming a good company into a great one. (The research is described in the sidebar "One Question, Five Years, 11 Companies.")

"Level 5" refers to the highest level in a hierarchy of executive capabilities that we identified during our research. Leaders at the other four levels in the hierarchy can produce high degrees of success but not enough to elevate companies from mediocrity to sustained excellence. (For more details about this concept, see the exhibit "The Level 5 Hierarchy.") And while Level 5 leadership is not the only

The Level 5 hierarchy

The Level 5 leader sits on top of a hierarchy of capabilities and is, according to our research, a necessary requirement for transforming an organization from good to great. But what lies beneath? Four other layers, each one appropriate in its own right but none with the power of Level 5. Individuals do not need to proceed sequentially through each level of the hierarchy to reach the top, but to be a full-fledged Level 5 requires the capabilities of all the lower levels, plus the special characteristics of Level 5.

Level 5

Executive: Builds enduring greatness through a paradoxical combination of personal humility plus professional will.

Level 4

Effective leader: Catalyzes commitment to and vigorous pursuit of a clear and compelling vision; stimulates the group to high performance standards.

Level 3

Competent manager: Organizes people and resources toward the effective and efficient pursuit of predetermined objectives.

Level 2

Contributing team member: Contributes to the achievement of group objectives; works effectively with others in a group setting.

Level 1

Highly capable individual: Makes productive contributions through talent, knowledge, skills, and good work habits.

Idea in Brief

Out of 1,435 *Fortune* 500 companies that renowned management researcher Jim Collins studied, only 11 achieved and sustained greatness—garnering stock returns at least three times the market's—for 15 years after a major transition period.

What did these 11 companies have in common? Each had a "Level 5" leader at the helm.

Level 5 leaders blend the paradoxical combination of **deep personal humility** with **intense professional will.** This rare combination also defies our assumptions about what makes a great leader.

Celebrities like Lee Iacocca may make headlines. But mild-mannered, steely leaders like Darwin Smith of Kimberly-Clark boost their companies to greatness—and keep them there.

Example: Darwin Smith—CEO at paper-products maker Kimberly-Clark from 1971 to 1991—epitomizes Level 5 leadership. Shy, awkward, shunning attention, he also showed iron will, determinedly redefining the firm's core business despite Wall Street's skepticism. The formerly lackluster Kimberly-Clark became the worldwide leader in its industry, generating stock returns 4.1 times greater than the general market's.

requirement for transforming a good company into a great one—other factors include getting the right people on the bus (and the wrong people off the bus) and creating a culture of discipline—our research shows it to be essential. Good-to-great transformations don't happen without Level 5 leaders at the helm. They just don't.

Not What You Would Expect

Our discovery of Level 5 leadership is counterintuitive. Indeed, it is countercultural. People generally assume that transforming companies from good to great requires larger-than-life leaders—big personalities like Lee Iacocca, Al Dunlap, Jack Welch, and Stanley Gault, who make headlines and become celebrities.

Compared with those CEOs, Darwin Smith seems to have come from Mars. Shy, unpretentious, even awkward, Smith shunned

Idea in Practice

Humility + Will = Level 5

How do Level 5 leaders manifest humility? They routinely credit others, external factors, and good luck for their companies' success. But when results are poor, they blame themselves. They also act quietly, calmly, and determinedly—relying on inspired standards, not inspiring charisma, to motivate.

Inspired standards demonstrate Level 5 leaders' unwavering will. Utterly intolerant of mediocrity, they are stoic in their resolve to do whatever it takes to produce great results—terminating everything else. And they select superb successors, wanting their companies to become even more successful in the future.

Can You Develop Level 5 Leadership?

Level 5 leaders sit atop a hierarchy of four more common leadership levels—and possess the skills of all four. For example, Level 4 leaders catalyze commitment to and vigorous pursuit of a clear, compelling vision. Can you move from Level 4 to Level 5? Perhaps, *if* you have the Level 5 "seed" within you.

Leaders *without* the seed tend to have monumental egos they can't subjugate to something larger and

attention. When a journalist asked him to describe his management style, Smith just stared back at the scribe from the other side of his thick black-rimmed glasses. He was dressed unfashionably, like a farm boy wearing his first J.C. Penney suit. Finally, after a long and uncomfortable silence, he said, "Eccentric." Needless to say, the *Wall Street Journal* did not publish a splashy feature on Darwin Smith.

But if you were to consider Smith soft or meek, you would be terribly mistaken. His lack of pretense was coupled with a fierce, even stoic, resolve toward life. Smith grew up on an Indiana farm and put himself through night school at Indiana University by working the day shift at International Harvester. One day, he lost a finger on the job. The story goes that he went to class that evening and returned to work the very next day. Eventually, this poor but determined Indiana farm boy earned admission to Harvard Law School.

Stockdale paradox

Deal with the brutal facts of your current reality—while maintaining absolute faith that you'll prevail.

Buildup-breakthrough flywheel

Keep pushing your organizational "flywheel." With consistent effort, momentum increases until— bang!—the wheel hits the break-through point.

The hedgehog concept

Think of your company as three in-tersecting circles: what it can be best at, how its economics work best, and what ignites its people's passions. Eliminate *everything* else.

more sustaining than themselves, i.e., their companies. But for leaders *with* the seed, the right conditions— such as self-reflection or a pro-foundly transformative event, such as a life-threatening illness—can stimulate the seed to sprout.

Growing to Level 5

Grow Level 5 seeds by practicing these good-to-great disciplines of Level 5 leaders.

First who

Attend to people first, strategy second. Get the right people on the bus and the wrong people off—*then* figure out where to drive it.

He showed the same iron will when he was at the helm of Kim-berly-Clark. Indeed, two months after Smith became CEO, doctors diagnosed him with nose and throat cancer and told him he had less than a year to live. He duly informed the board of his illness but said he had no plans to die anytime soon. Smith held to his demanding work schedule while commuting weekly from Wisconsin to Houston for radiation therapy. He lived 25 more years, 20 of them as CEO.

Smith's ferocious resolve was crucial to the rebuilding of Kimberly-Clark, especially when he made the most dramatic deci-sion in the company's history: selling the mills.

To explain: Shortly after he took over, Smith and his team had concluded that the company's traditional core business—coated paper—was doomed to mediocrity. Its economics were bad and the competition weak. But, they reasoned, if Kimberly-Clark were thrust into the fire of the consumer paper products business, better

One Question, Five Years, 11 Companies

THE LEVEL 5 DISCOVERY DERIVES from a research project that began in 1996, when my research teams and I set out to answer one question: Can a good company become a great company and, if so, how? Most great companies grew up with superb parents—people like George Merck, David Packard, and Walt Disney—who instilled greatness early on. But what about the vast majority of companies that wake up partway through life and realize that they're good but not great?

To answer that question, we looked for companies that had shifted from good performance to great performance—and sustained it. We identified comparison companies that had failed to make that sustained shift. We then studied the contrast between the two groups to discover common variables that distinguished those who made and sustained a shift from those who could have but didn't.

More precisely, we searched for a specific pattern: cumulative stock returns at or below the general stock market for 15 years, punctuated by a transition point, then cumulative returns at least three times the market over the next 15 years. (See the accompanying exhibit.) We used data from the University of Chicago Center for Research in Security Prices and adjusted for stock splits and all dividends reinvested. The shift had to be distinct from the industry; if the whole industry showed the same shift, we'd drop the company. We began with 1,435 companies that appeared on the *Fortune* 500 from 1965 to 1995; we found 11 good-to-great examples. That's not a sample; that's the total number that jumped all our hurdles and passed into the study.

Those that made the cut averaged cumulative stock returns 6.9 times the general stock market for the 15 years after the point of transition. To put that in perspective, General Electric under Jack Welch outperformed the general stock market by 2.8:1 during his tenure from 1986 to 2000. One dollar invested in a mutual fund of the good-to-great companies in 1965 grew to $470 by 2000 compared with $56 in the general stock market. These are remarkable numbers, made all the more so by the fact that they came from previously unremarkable companies.

For each good-to-great example, we selected the best direct comparison, based on similarity of business, size, age, customers, and performance leading up to the transition. We also constructed a set of six "unsustained" comparisons (companies that showed a short-lived shift but then fell off) to address the question of sustainability. To be conservative, we consistently picked comparison companies that, if anything, were in better shape than the good-to-great companies were in the years just before the transition.

With 22 research associates working in groups of four to six at a time from 1996 to 2000, our study involved a wide range of both qualitative and quantitative analyses. On the qualitative front, we collected nearly 6,000 articles, conducted 87 interviews with key executives, analyzed companies' internal strategy documents, and culled through analysts' reports. On the quantitative front, we ran financial metrics, examined executive compensation, compared patterns of management turnover, quantified company layoffs and restructurings, and calculated the effect of acquisitions and divestitures on companies' stocks. We then synthesized the results to identify the drivers of good-to-great transformations. One was Level 5 leadership. (The others are described in the sidebar "Not by Level 5 Alone.")

Since only 11 companies qualified as good-to-great, a research finding had to meet a stiff standard before we would deem it significant. Every component in the final framework showed up in all 11 good-to-great companies during the transition era, regardless of industry (from steel to banking), transition decade (from the 1950s to the 1990s), circumstances (from plodding along to dire crisis), or size (from tens of millions to tens of billions). Additionally, every component had to show up in less than 30% of the comparison companies during the relevant years. Level 5 easily made it into the framework as one of the strongest, most consistent contrasts between the good-to-great and the comparison companies.

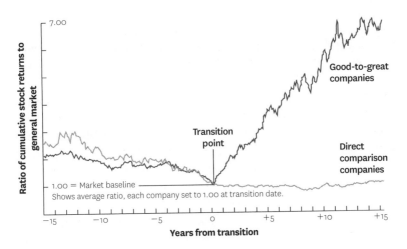

economics and world-class competition like Procter & Gamble would force it to achieve greatness or perish.

And so, like the general who burned the boats upon landing on enemy soil, leaving his troops to succeed or die, Smith announced that Kimberly-Clark would sell its mills—even the namesake mill in Kimberly, Wisconsin. All proceeds would be thrown into the consumer business, with investments in brands like Huggies diapers and Kleenex tissues. The business media called the move stupid, and Wall Street analysts downgraded the stock. But Smith never wavered. Twenty-five years later, Kimberly-Clark owned Scott Paper and beat Procter & Gamble in six of eight product categories. In retirement, Smith reflected on his exceptional performance, saying simply, "I never stopped trying to become qualified for the job."

Not What We Expected, Either

We'll look in depth at Level 5 leadership, but first let's set an important context for our findings. We were not looking for Level 5 or anything like it. Our original question was, Can a good company become a great one and, if so, how? In fact, I gave the research teams explicit instructions to downplay the role of top executives in their analyses of this question so we wouldn't slip into the simplistic "credit the leader" or "blame the leader" thinking that is so common today.

But Level 5 found us. Over the course of the study, research teams kept saying, "We can't ignore the top executives even if we want to. There is something consistently unusual about them." I would push back, arguing, "The comparison companies also had leaders. So what's different here?" Back and forth the debate raged. Finally, as should always be the case, the data won. The executives at companies that went from good to great and sustained that performance for 15 years or more were all cut from the same cloth—one remarkably different from that which produced the executives at the comparison companies in our study. It didn't matter whether the company was in crisis or steady state, consumer or industrial, offering services or products. It didn't matter when the transition took place or how big the company. The successful organizations all had a Level 5 leader at the time of transition.

Furthermore, the absence of Level 5 leadership showed up consistently across the comparison companies. The point: Level 5 is an empirical finding, not an ideological one. And that's important to note, given how much the Level 5 finding contradicts not only conventional wisdom but much of management theory to date. (For more about our findings on good-to-great transformations, see the sidebar "Not by Level 5 Alone.")

Humility + Will = Level 5

Level 5 leaders are a study in duality: modest and willful, shy and fearless. To grasp this concept, consider Abraham Lincoln, who never let his ego get in the way of his ambition to create an enduring great nation. Author Henry Adams called him "a quiet, peaceful, shy figure." But those who thought Lincoln's understated manner signaled weakness in the man found themselves terribly mistaken—to the scale of 250,000 Confederate and 360,000 Union lives, including Lincoln's own.

It might be a stretch to compare the 11 Level 5 CEOs in our research to Lincoln, but they did display the same kind of duality. Take Colman M. Mockler, CEO of Gillette from 1975 to 1991. Mockler, who faced down three takeover attempts, was a reserved, gracious man with a gentle, almost patrician manner. Despite epic battles with raiders—he took on Ronald Perelman twice and the former Coniston Partners once—he never lost his shy, courteous style. At the height of crisis, he maintained a calm business-as-usual demeanor, dispensing first with ongoing business before turning to the takeover.

And yet, those who mistook Mockler's outward modesty as a sign of inner weakness were beaten in the end. In one proxy battle, Mockler and other senior executives called thousands of investors, one by one, to win their votes. Mockler simply would not give in. He chose to fight for the future greatness of Gillette even though he could have pocketed millions by flipping his stock.

Not by Level 5 Alone

Level 5 leadership is an essential factor for taking a company from good to great, but it's not the only one. Our research uncovered multiple factors that deliver companies to greatness. And it is the combined package—Level 5 plus these other drivers—that takes companies beyond unremarkable. There is a symbiotic relationship between Level 5 and the rest of our findings: Level 5 enables implementation of the other findings, and practicing the other findings may help you get to Level 5. We've already talked about who Level 5 leaders are; the rest of our findings describe what they do. Here is a brief look at some of the other key findings.

First Who

We expected that good-to-great leaders would start with the vision and strategy. Instead, they attended to people first, strategy second. They got the right people on the bus, moved the wrong people off, ushered the right people to the right seats—and then they figured out where to drive it.

Stockdale Paradox

This finding is named after Admiral James Stockdale, winner of the Medal of Honor, who survived seven years in a Vietcong POW camp by hanging on to two contradictory beliefs:

His life couldn't be worse at the moment, and his life would someday be better than ever. Like Stockdale, people at the good-to-great companies in our research confronted the most brutal facts of their current reality, yet simultaneously maintained absolute faith that they would prevail in the end. And they held both disciplines—faith and facts—at the same time, all the time.

Buildup-Breakthrough Flywheel

Good-to-great transformations do not happen overnight or in one big leap. Rather, the process resembles relentlessly pushing a giant, heavy flywheel in one direction. At first, pushing it gets the flywheel to turn once. With consistent effort, it goes two turns, then five, then ten, building increasing momentum until—bang!—the wheel hits the breakthrough point, and the momentum

Consider the consequences had Mockler capitulated. If a share flipper had accepted the full 44% price premium offered by Perelman and then invested those shares in the general market for ten years, he still would have come out 64% behind a shareholder who stayed with Mockler and Gillette. If Mockler had given up the fight, really kicks in. Our comparison companies never sustained the kind of breakthrough momentum that the good-to-great companies did; instead, they lurched back and forth with radical change programs, reactionary moves, and restructurings.

The Hedgehog Concept

In a famous essay, philosopher and scholar Isaiah Berlin described two approaches to thought and life using a simple parable: The fox knows a little about many things, but the hedgehog knows only one big thing very well. The fox is complex; the hedgehog simple. And the hedgehog wins. Our research shows that breakthroughs require a simple, hedgehog-like understanding of three intersecting circles: what a company can be the best in the world at, how its economics work best, and what best ignites the passions of its people. Breakthroughs happen when you get the hedgehog concept and become systematic and consistent with it, eliminating virtually anything that does not fit in the three circles.

Technology Accelerators

The good-to-great companies had a paradoxical relationship with technology. On the one hand, they assiduously avoided jumping on new technology bandwagons. On the other, they were pioneers in the application of carefully selected technologies, making bold, farsighted investments in those that directly linked to their hedgehog concept. Like turbochargers, these technology accelerators create an explosion in flywheel momentum.

A Culture of Discipline

When you look across the good-to-great transformations, they consistently display three forms of discipline: disciplined people, disciplined thought, and disciplined action. When you have disciplined people, you don't need hierarchy. When you have disciplined thought, you don't need bureaucracy. When you have disciplined action, you don't need excessive controls. When you combine a culture of discipline with an ethic of entrepreneurship, you get the magical alchemy of great performance.

---

it's likely that none of us would be shaving with Sensor, Lady Sensor, or the Mach III—and hundreds of millions of people would have a more painful battle with daily stubble.

Sadly, Mockler never had the chance to enjoy the full fruits of his efforts. In January 1991, Gillette received an advance copy of *Forbes*.

The cover featured an artist's rendition of the publicity-shy Mockler standing on a mountaintop, holding a giant razor above his head in a triumphant pose. Walking back to his office just minutes after seeing this public acknowledgment of his 16 years of struggle, Mockler crumpled to the floor and died of a massive heart attack.

Even if Mockler had known he would die in office, he could not have changed his approach. His placid persona hid an inner intensity, a dedication to making anything he touched the best—not just because of what he would get but because he couldn't imagine doing it any other way. Mockler could not give up the company to those who would destroy it, any more than Lincoln would risk losing the chance to build an enduring great nation.

A Compelling Modesty

The Mockler story illustrates the modesty typical of Level 5 leaders. (For a summary of Level 5 traits, see the exhibit "The Yin and Yang of Level 5.") Indeed, throughout our interviews with such executives, we were struck by the way they talked about themselves—or rather, didn't talk about themselves. They'd go on and on about the company and the contributions of other executives, but they would instinctively deflect discussion about their own role. When pressed to talk about themselves, they'd say things like, "I hope I'm not sounding like a big shot," or "I don't think I can take much credit for what happened. We were blessed with marvelous people." One Level 5 leader even asserted, "There are a lot of people in this company who could do my job better than I do."

By contrast, consider the courtship of personal celebrity by the comparison CEOs. Scott Paper, the comparison company to Kimberly-Clark, hired Al Dunlap as CEO—a man who would tell anyone who would listen (and many who would have preferred not to) about his accomplishments. After 19 months atop Scott Paper, Dunlap said in *BusinessWeek,* "The Scott story will go down in the annals of American business history as one of the most successful, quickest turnarounds ever. It makes other turnarounds pale by comparison." He personally accrued $100 million for 603 days of work at Scott

---

The Yin and Yang of Level 5

Personal humility

Demonstrates a compelling modesty, shunning public adulation; never boastful.

Acts with quiet, calm determination; relies principally on inspired standards, not inspiring charisma, to motivate.

Channels ambition into the company, not the self; sets up successors for even more greatness in the next generation.

Looks in the mirror, not out the window, to apportion responsibility for poor results, never blaming other people, external factors, or bad luck.

Professional will

Creates superb results, a clear catalyst in the transition from good to great.

Demonstrates an unwavering resolve to do whatever must be done to produce the best long-term results, no matter how difficult.

Sets the standard of building an enduring great company; will settle for nothing less.

Looks out the window, not in the mirror, to apportion credit for the success of the company—to other people, external factors, and good luck.

Paper—about $165,000 per day—largely by slashing the workforce, halving the R&D budget, and putting the company on growth steroids in preparation for sale. After selling off the company and pocketing his quick millions, Dunlap wrote an autobiography in which he boastfully dubbed himself "Rambo in pinstripes." It's hard to imagine Darwin Smith thinking, "Hey, that Rambo character reminds me of me," let alone stating it publicly.

Granted, the Scott Paper story is one of the more dramatic in our study, but it's not an isolated case. In more than two-thirds of the comparison companies, we noted the presence of a gargantuan ego that contributed to the demise or continued mediocrity of the company. We found this pattern particularly strong in the unsustained comparison companies—the companies that would show a shift in performance under a talented yet egocentric Level 4 leader, only to decline in later years.

Lee Iacocca, for example, saved Chrysler from the brink of catastrophe, performing one of the most celebrated (and deservedly so) turnarounds in U.S. business history. The automaker's stock rose 2.9 times higher than the general market about halfway through his tenure. But then Iacocca diverted his attention to transforming himself. He appeared regularly on talk shows like the *Today Show* and *Larry King Live,* starred in more than 80 commercials, entertained the idea of running for president of the United States, and promoted his autobiography, which sold 7 million copies worldwide. Iacocca's personal stock soared, but Chrysler's stock fell 31% below the market in the second half of his tenure.

And once Iacocca had accumulated all the fame and perks, he found it difficult to leave center stage. He postponed his retirement so many times that Chrysler's insiders began to joke that Iacocca stood for "I Am Chairman of Chrysler Corporation Always." When he finally retired, he demanded that the board continue to provide a private jet and stock options. Later, he joined forces with noted takeover artist Kirk Kerkorian to launch a hostile bid for Chrysler. (It failed.) Iacocca did make one final brilliant decision: He picked a modest yet determined man—perhaps even a Level 5—as his successor. Bob Eaton rescued Chrysler from its second near-death crisis in a decade and set the foundation for a more enduring corporate transition.

An Unwavering Resolve

Besides extreme humility, Level 5 leaders also display tremendous professional will. When George Cain became CEO of Abbott Laboratories, it was a drowsy, family-controlled business sitting at the bottom quartile of the pharmaceutical industry, living off its cash cow, erythromycin. Cain was a typical Level 5 leader in his lack of pretense; he didn't have the kind of inspiring personality that would galvanize the company. But he had something much more powerful: inspired standards. He could not stand mediocrity in any form and was utterly intolerant of anyone who would accept the idea that good is good enough. For the next 14 years, he relentlessly imposed his will for greatness on Abbott Labs.

Among Cain's first tasks was to destroy one of the root causes of Abbott's middling performance: nepotism. By systematically rebuilding both the board and the executive team with the best people he could find, Cain made his statement. Family ties no longer mattered. If you couldn't become the best executive in the industry within your span of responsibility, you would lose your paycheck.

Such near-ruthless rebuilding might be expected from an outsider brought in to turn the company around, but Cain was an 18-year insider—and a part of the family, the son of a previous president. Holiday gatherings were probably tense for a few years in the Cain clan—"Sorry I had to fire you. Want another slice of turkey?"—but in the end, family members were pleased with the performance of their stock. Cain had set in motion a profitable growth machine. From its transition in 1974 to 2000, Abbott created shareholder returns that beat the market 4.5:1, outperforming industry superstars Merck and Pfizer by a factor of two.

Another good example of iron-willed Level 5 leadership comes from Charles R. "Cork" Walgreen III, who transformed dowdy Walgreens into a company that outperformed the stock market 16:1 from its transition in 1975 to 2000. After years of dialogue and debate within his executive team about what to do with Walgreens' food-service operations, this CEO sensed the team had finally reached a watershed: The company's brightest future lay in convenient drugstores, not in food service. Dan Jorndt, who succeeded Walgreen in 1988, describes what happened next:

Cork said at one of our planning committee meetings, "Okay, now I am going to draw the line in the sand. We are going to be out of the restaurant business completely in five years." At the time we had more than 500 restaurants. You could have heard a pin drop. He said, "I want to let everybody know the clock is ticking." Six months later we were at our next planning committee meeting and someone mentioned just in passing that we had only five years to be out of the restaurant business. Cork was not a real vociferous fellow. He sort of tapped on the table and said, "Listen, you now have four-and-a-half years. I said you had five years six months ago. Now you've got four-and-a-half years." Well, that next day things really clicked into gear for winding down our restaurant business. Cork never wavered. He never doubted. He never second-guessed.

Like Darwin Smith selling the mills at Kimberly-Clark, Cork Walgreen required stoic resolve to make his decisions. Food service was not the largest part of the business, although it did add substantial profits to the bottom line. The real problem was more emotional than financial. Walgreens had, after all, invented the malted milk shake, and food service had been a long-standing family tradition dating back to Cork's grandfather. Not only that, some food-service outlets were even named after the CEO—for example, a restaurant chain named Corky's. But no matter; if Walgreen had to fly in the face of family tradition in order to refocus on the one arena in which Walgreens could be the best in the world—convenient drugstores— and terminate everything else that would not produce great results, then Cork would do it. Quietly, doggedly, simply.

One final, yet compelling, note on our findings about Level 5: Because Level 5 leaders have ambition not for themselves but for their companies, they routinely select superb successors. Level 5 leaders want to see their companies become even more successful in the next generation and are comfortable with the idea that most people won't even know that the roots of that success trace back to them. As one Level 5 CEO said, "I want to look from my porch, see the company as one of the great companies in the world someday, and be able to say, 'I used to work there.'" By contrast, Level 4 leaders often fail to set up the company for enduring success. After all, what better testament to your own personal greatness than that the place falls apart after you leave?

In more than three-quarters of the comparison companies, we found executives who set up their successors for failure, chose weak successors, or both. Consider the case of Rubbermaid, which grew from obscurity to become one of *Fortune*'s most admired companies—and then, just as quickly, disintegrated into such sorry shape that it had to be acquired by Newell.

The architect of this remarkable story was a charismatic and brilliant leader named Stanley C. Gault, whose name became synonymous in the late 1980s with Rubbermaid's success. Across the 312 articles collected by our research team about the company, Gault comes through as a hard-driving, egocentric executive. In one article, he responds to the accusation of being a tyrant with the statement, "Yes, but I'm a sincere tyrant." In another, drawn directly from his own comments on leading change, the word "I" appears 44 times, while the word "we" appears 16 times. Of course, Gault had every reason to be proud of his executive success: Rubbermaid generated 40 consecutive quarters of earnings growth under his leadership—an impressive performance, to be sure, and one that deserves respect.

But Gault did not leave behind a company that would be great without him. His chosen successor lasted a year on the job and the next in line faced a management team so shallow that he had to temporarily shoulder four jobs while scrambling to identify a new number-two executive. Gault's successors struggled not only with a management void but also with strategic voids that would eventually bring the company to its knees.

Of course, you might say—as one *Fortune* article did—that the fact that Rubbermaid fell apart after Gault left proves his greatness as a leader. Gault was a tremendous Level 4 leader, perhaps one of the best in the last 50 years. But he was not at Level 5, and that is one crucial reason why Rubbermaid went from good to great for a brief, shining moment and then just as quickly went from great to irrelevant.

The Window and the Mirror

As part of our research, we interviewed Alan L. Wurtzel, the Level 5 leader responsible for turning Circuit City from a ramshackle company on the edge of bankruptcy into one of America's most successful electronics retailers. In the 15 years after its transition date in 1982, Circuit City outperformed the market 18.5:1.

We asked Wurtzel to list the top five factors in his company's transformation, ranked by importance. His number one factor? Luck. "We were in a great industry, with the wind at our backs," he said. But wait a minute, we retorted, Silo—your comparison company—was in the same industry, with the same wind and bigger sails. The conversation went back and forth, with Wurtzel refusing to take much credit for the transition, preferring to attribute it largely to just being in the right place at the right time. Later, when we asked him to discuss the factors that would sustain a good-to-great transformation, he said, "The first thing that comes to mind is luck. I was lucky to find the right successor."

Luck. What an odd factor to talk about. Yet the Level 5 leaders we identified invoked it frequently. We asked an executive at steel company Nucor why it had such a remarkable track record for making good decisions. His response? "I guess we were just lucky." Joseph F. Cullman III, the Level 5 CEO of Philip Morris, flat out refused to take credit for his company's success, citing his good fortune to have great colleagues, successors, and predecessors. Even the book he wrote about his career—which he penned at the urging of his colleagues and which he never intended to distribute widely outside the company—had the unusual title *I'm a Lucky Guy*.

At first, we were puzzled by the Level 5 leaders' emphasis on good luck. After all, there is no evidence that the companies that had progressed from good to great were blessed with more good luck (or more bad luck, for that matter) than the comparison companies. But then we began to notice an interesting pattern in the executives at the comparison companies: They often blamed their situations on bad luck, bemoaning the difficulties of the environment they faced.

Compare Bethlehem Steel and Nucor, for example. Both steel companies operated with products that are hard to differentiate, and both faced a competitive challenge from cheap imported steel. Both companies paid significantly higher wages than most of their foreign competitors. And yet executives at the two companies held completely different views of the same environment.

Bethlehem Steel's CEO summed up the company's problems in 1983 by blaming the imports: "Our first, second, and third problems are imports." Meanwhile, Ken Iverson and his crew at Nucor saw the imports as a blessing: "Aren't we lucky; steel is heavy, and they have to ship it all the way across the ocean, giving us a huge advantage." Indeed, Iverson saw the first, second, and third problems facing the U.S. steel industry not in imports but in management. He even went so far as to speak out publicly against government protection against imports, telling a gathering of stunned steel executives in 1977 that the real problems facing the industry lay in the fact that management had failed to keep pace with technology.

The emphasis on luck turns out to be part of a broader pattern that we have come to call "the window and the mirror." Level 5 leaders, inherently humble, look out the window to apportion credit—even undue credit—to factors outside themselves. If they can't find a specific person or event to give credit to, they credit good luck. At the same time, they look in the mirror to assign responsibility, never citing bad luck or external factors when things go poorly. Conversely, the comparison executives frequently looked out the window for factors to blame but preened in the mirror to credit themselves when things went well.

The funny thing about the window-and-mirror concept is that it does not reflect reality. According to our research, the Level 5 leaders were responsible for their companies' transformations. But they would never admit that. We can't climb inside their heads and assess whether they deeply believed what they saw through the window and in the mirror. But it doesn't really matter, because they acted as if they believed it, and they acted with such consistency that it produced exceptional results.

Born or Bred?

Not long ago, I shared the Level 5 finding with a gathering of senior executives. A woman who had recently become chief executive of her company raised her hand. "I believe what you've told us about Level 5 leadership," she said, "but I'm disturbed because I know I'm not there yet, and maybe I never will be. Part of the reason I got this job is because of my strong ego. Are you telling me that I can't make my company great if I'm not Level 5?"

"Let me return to the data," I responded. "Of 1,435 companies that appeared on the *Fortune* 500 since 1965, only 11 made it into our study. In those 11, all of them had Level 5 leaders in key positions, including the CEO role, at the pivotal time of transition. Now, to reiterate, we're not saying that Level 5 is the only element required for the move from good to great, but it appears to be essential."

She sat there, quiet for a moment, and you could guess what many people in the room were thinking. Finally, she raised her hand again. "Can you learn to become Level 5?" I still do not know the answer to that question. Our research, frankly, did not delve into how Level 5 leaders come to be, nor did we attempt to explain or codify the nature of their emotional lives. We speculated on the unique psychology of Level 5 leaders. Were they "guilty" of displacement—shifting their own raw ambition onto something other than themselves? Were they sublimating their egos for dark and complex reasons rooted in childhood trauma? Who knows? And perhaps more important, do the psychological roots of Level 5 leadership matter any more than do the roots of charisma or intelligence? The question remains: Can Level 5 be developed?

My preliminary hypothesis is that there are two categories of people: those who don't have the Level 5 seed within them and those who do. The first category consists of people who could never in a million years bring themselves to subjugate their own needs to the greater ambition of something larger and more lasting than themselves. For those people, work will always be first and foremost about what they get—the fame, fortune, power, adulation, and so on. Work will never be about what they build, create, and contribute. The great irony is that the animus and personal ambition that often drives people to become a Level 4 leader stands at odds with the humility required to rise to Level 5.

When you combine that irony with the fact that boards of directors frequently operate under the false belief that a larger-than-life, egocentric leader is required to make a company great, you can quickly see why Level 5 leaders rarely appear at the top of our institutions. We keep putting people in positions of power who lack the seed to become a Level 5 leader, and that is one major reason why there are so few companies that make a sustained and verifiable shift from good to great.

The second category consists of people who could evolve to Level 5; the capability resides within them, perhaps buried or ignored or simply nascent. Under the right circumstances—with self-reflection, a mentor, loving parents, a significant life experience, or other factors—the seed can begin to develop. Some of the Level 5 leaders in our study had significant life experiences that might have sparked development of the seed. Darwin Smith fully blossomed as a Level 5 after his near-death experience with cancer. Joe Cullman was profoundly affected by his World War II experiences, particularly the last-minute change of orders that took him off a doomed ship on which he surely would have died; he considered the next 60-odd years a great gift. A strong religious belief or conversion might also nurture the seed. Colman Mockler, for example, converted to evangelical Christianity while getting his MBA at Harvard, and later, according to the book *Cutting Edge* by Gordon McKibben, he became a prime mover in a group of Boston business executives that met frequently over breakfast to discuss the carryover of religious values to corporate life.

We would love to be able to give you a list of steps for getting to Level 5—other than contracting cancer, going through a religious conversion, or getting different parents—but we have no solid research data that would support a credible list. Our research exposed Level 5 as a key component inside the black box of what it takes to shift a company from good to great. Yet inside that black box is another—the inner development of a person to Level 5 leadership. We could speculate on what that inner box might hold, but it would mostly be just that: speculation.

In short, Level 5 is a very satisfying idea, a truthful idea, a powerful idea, and, to make the move from good to great, very likely an essential idea. But to provide "ten steps to Level 5 leadership" would trivialize the concept.

My best advice, based on the research, is to practice the other good-to-great disciplines that we discovered. Since we found a tight symbiotic relationship between each of the other findings and Level 5, we suspect that conscientiously trying to lead using the other disciplines can help you move in the right direction. There is no guarantee that doing so will turn executives into full-fledged Level 5 leaders, but it gives them a tangible place to begin, especially if they have the seed within.

We cannot say for sure what percentage of people have the seed within, nor how many of those can nurture it enough to become

Level 5. Even those of us on the research team who identified Level 5 do not know whether we will succeed in evolving to its heights. And yet all of us who worked on the finding have been inspired by the idea of trying to move toward Level 5. Darwin Smith, Colman Mockler, Alan Wurtzel, and all the other Level 5 leaders we learned about have become role models for us. Whether or not we make it to Level 5, it is worth trying. For like all basic truths about what is best in human beings, when we catch a glimpse of that truth, we know that our own lives and all that we touch will be the better for making the effort to get there.

Originally published in January 2001. Reprint R0507M

Seven Transformations of Leadership

by David Rooke and William R. Torbert

MOST DEVELOPMENTAL PSYCHOLOGISTS agree that what differentiates leaders is not so much their philosophy of leadership, their personality, or their style of management. Rather, it's their internal "action logic"—how they interpret their surroundings and react when their power or safety is challenged. Relatively few leaders, however, try to understand their own action logic, and fewer still have explored the possibility of changing it.

They should, because we've found that leaders who do undertake a voyage of personal understanding and development can transform not only their own capabilities but also those of their companies. In our close collaboration with psychologist Susanne Cook-Greuter—and our 25 years of extensive survey-based consulting at companies such as Deutsche Bank, Harvard Pilgrim Health Care, Hewlett-Packard, NSA, Trillium Asset Management, Aviva, and Volvo—we've worked with thousands of executives as they've tried to develop their leadership skills. The good news is that leaders who make an effort to understand their own action logic can improve their ability to lead. But to do that, it's important first to understand what kind of leader you already are.

The Seven Action Logics

Our research is based on a sentence-completion survey tool called the Leadership Development Profile. Using this tool, participants are asked to complete 36 sentences that begin with phrases such as "A good leader . . . ," to which responses vary widely:

". . . cracks the whip."

". . . realizes that it's important to achieve good performance from subordinates."

". . . juggles competing forces and takes responsibility for her decisions."

By asking participants to complete sentences of this type, it's possible for highly trained evaluators to paint a picture of how participants interpret their own actions and the world around them; these "pictures" show which one of seven developmental action logics—Opportunist, Diplomat, Expert, Achiever, Individualist, Strategist, or Alchemist—currently functions as a leader's dominant way of thinking. Leaders can move through these categories as their abilities grow, so taking the Leadership Development Profile again several years later can reveal whether a leader's action logic has evolved.

Over the past 25 years, we and other researchers have administered the sentence-completion survey to thousands of managers and professionals, most between the ages of 25 and 55, at hundreds of American and European companies (as well as nonprofits and governmental agencies) in diverse industries. What we found is that the levels of corporate and individual performance vary according to action logic. Notably, we found that the three types of leaders associated with below-average corporate performance (Opportunists, Diplomats, and Experts) accounted for 55% of our sample. They were significantly less effective at implementing organizational strategies than the 30% of the sample who measured as Achievers. Moreover, only the final 15% of managers in the sample (Individualists, Strategists, and Alchemists) showed the consistent capacity to innovate and to successfully transform their organizations.

Idea in Brief

Every company needs transformational leaders—those who spearhead changes that elevate profitability, expand market share, and change the rules of the game in their industry. But few executives understand the unique strengths needed to become such a leader. Result? They miss the opportunity to develop those strengths. They and their firms lose out.

How to avoid this scenario? Recognize that great leaders are differentiated not by their personality or philosophy but by their **action logic**—how they interpret their own and others' behavior and how they maintain power or protect against threats.

Some leaders rely on action logics that hinder organizational performance. Opportunists, for example, believe in winning any way possible, and often exploit others to score personal gains. Few people follow them for long. Other types prove potent change agents. In particular, Strategists believe that every aspect of their organization is open to discussion and transformation. Their action logic enables them to challenge perceptions that constrain their organizations and to overcome resistance to change. They create compelling, shared visions and lead the pragmatic initiatives needed to realize those visions.

Though Strategists are rare, you *can* develop their defining strengths. How? Diagnose your current action logic and work to upgrade it. The payoff? You help your company execute the changes it needs to excel.

To understand how leaders fall into such distinct categories and corporate performance, let's look in more detail at each leadership style in turn, starting with the least productive (and least complex).

The Opportunist

Our most comforting finding was that only 5% of the leaders in our sample were characterized by mistrust, egocentrism, and manipulativeness. We call these leaders Opportunists, a title that reflects their tendency to focus on personal wins and see the world and other

Idea in Practice

Seven Types of Action Logic

Type	Characteristics	Strengths	Weaknesses
Opportunist	*Wins any way possible.* Self-oriented; manipulative; "might makes right."	Good in emergencies and in pursuing sales.	Few people want to follow them for the long term.
Diplomat	*Avoids conflict.* Wants to belong; obeys group norms; doesn't rock the boat.	Supportive glue on teams.	Can't provide painful feedback or make the hard decisions needed to improve performance.
Expert	*Rules by logic and expertise.* Uses hard data to gain consensus and buy-in.	Good individual contributor.	Lacks emotional intelligence; lacks respect for those with less expertise.
Achiever	*Meets strategic goals.* Promotes teamwork; juggles managerial duties and responds to market demands to achieve goals.	Well suited to managerial work.	Inhibits thinking outside the box.
Individualist	*Operates in unconventional ways.* Ignores rules he/she regards as irrelevant.	Effective in venture and consulting roles.	Irritates colleagues and bosses by ignoring key organizational processes and people.
Strategist	*Generates organizational and personal change.* Highly collaborative; weaves visions with pragmatic, timely initiatives; challenges existing assumptions.	Generates transformations over the short and long term.	None
Alchemist	*Generates social transformations (e.g., Nelson Mandela).* Reinvents organizations in historically significant ways.	Leads societywide change.	None

Changing Your Action Logic Type

To change your action logic type, experiment with new interpersonal behaviors, forge new kinds of relationships, and seize advantage of work opportunities. For example:

To advance from. . .	Take these steps
Expert to Achiever	Focus more on delivering results than on perfecting your knowledge: • Become aware of differences between your assumptions and those of others. For example, practice new conversational strategies such as "You may be right, but I'd like to understand what leads you to believe that." • Participate in training programs on topics such as effective delegation and leading high-performing teams
Achiever to Individualist	Instead of accepting goals as givens to be achieved: • Reflect on the worth of the goals themselves, with the aim of improving future goals • Use annual leadership development planning to thoughtfully set the highest-impact goals
Individualist to Strategist	Engage in peer-to-peer development: • Establish mutual mentoring with members of your professional network (board members, top managers, industry leaders) who can challenge your assumptions and practices, as well as those of your company and industry. *Example:* One CEO of a dental hygiene company envisioned introducing affordable dental hygiene in developing countries. He explored the idea with colleagues across the country, eventually proposing an educational and charitable venture that his parent company agreed to fund. He was promoted to a new vice presidency for international ventures within the parent company.

people as opportunities to be exploited. Their approach to the outside world is largely determined by their perception of control—in other words, how they will react to an event depends primarily on whether or not they think they can direct the outcome. They treat other people as objects or as competitors who are also out for themselves.

Opportunists tend to regard their bad behavior as legitimate in the cut and thrust of an eye-for-an-eye world. They reject feedback, externalize blame, and retaliate harshly. One can see this action logic in the early work of Larry Ellison (now CEO of Oracle). Ellison describes his managerial style at the start of his career as "management by ridicule." "You've got to be good at intellectual intimidation and rhetorical bullying," he once told Matthew Symonds of the *Economist*. "I'd excuse my behavior by telling myself I was just having 'an open and honest debate.' The fact is, I just didn't know any better."

Few Opportunists remain managers for long, unless they transform to more effective action logics (as Ellison has done). Their constant firefighting, their style of self-aggrandizement, and their frequent rule breaking is the antithesis of the kind of leader people want to work with for the long term. If you have worked for an Opportunist, you will almost certainly remember it as a difficult time. By the same token, corporate environments that breed opportunism seldom endure, although Opportunists often survive longer than they should because they provide an exciting environment in which younger executives, especially, can take risks. As one ex-Enron senior staffer said, "Before the fall, those were such exciting years. We felt we could do anything, pull off everything, write our own rules. The pace was wild, and we all just rode it." Of course, Enron's shareholders and pensioners would reasonably feel that they were paying too heavily for that staffer's adventure.

The Diplomat

The Diplomat makes sense of the world around him in a more benign way than the Opportunist does, but this action logic can also have extremely negative repercussions if the leader is a senior manager.

Loyally serving the group, the Diplomat seeks to please higher-status colleagues while avoiding conflict. This action logic is focused on gaining control of one's own behavior—more than on gaining control of external events or other people. According to the Diplomat's action logic, a leader gains more enduring acceptance and influence by cooperating with group norms and by performing his daily roles well.

In a support role or a team context, this type of executive has much to offer. Diplomats provide social glue to their colleagues and ensure that attention is paid to the needs of others, which is probably why the great majority of Diplomats work at the most junior rungs of management, in jobs such as frontline supervisor, customer service representative, or nurse practitioner. Indeed, research into 497 managers in different industries showed that 80% of all Diplomats were at junior levels. By contrast, 80% of all Strategists were at senior levels, suggesting that managers who grow into more effective action logics—like that of the Strategist—have a greater chance of being promoted.

Diplomats are much more problematic in top leadership roles because they try to ignore conflict. They tend to be overly polite and friendly and find it virtually impossible to give challenging feedback to others. Initiating change, with its inevitable conflicts, represents a grave threat to the Diplomat, and he will avoid it if at all possible, even to the point of self-destruction.

Consider one Diplomat who became the interim CEO of an organization when his predecessor died suddenly from an aneurysm. When the board split on the selection of a permanent successor, it asked the Diplomat to carry on. Our Diplomat relished his role as a ceremonial figurehead and was a sought-after speaker at public events. Unfortunately, he found the more conflictual requirements of the job less to his liking. He failed, for instance, to replace a number of senior managers who had serious ongoing performance issues and were resisting the change program his predecessor had initiated. Because the changes were controversial, the Diplomat avoided meetings, even planning business trips for the times when the senior team would meet. The team members were so frustrated by the Diplomat's attitude that they eventually resigned en masse. He "resolved" this

Seven Ways of Leading

DIFFERENT LEADERS exhibit different kinds of action logic—ways in which they interpret their surroundings and react when their power or safety is challenged. In our research of thousands of leaders, we observed seven types of action logics. The least effective for organizational leadership are the Opportunist and Diplomat; the most effective, the Strategist and Alchemist. Knowing your own action logic can be the first step toward developing a more effective leadership style. If you recognize yourself as an Individualist, for example, you can work, through both formal and informal measures, to develop the strengths and characteristics of a Strategist.

Action Logic	Characteristics	Strengths	% of research sample profiling at this action logic
Opportunist	*Wins any way possible.* Self-oriented; manipulative; "might makes right."	Good in emergencies and in sales opportunities.	5%
Diplomat	*Avoids overt conflict.* Wants to belong; obeys group norms; rarely rocks the boat.	Good as supportive glue within an office; helps bring people together.	12%
Expert	*Rules by logic and expertise.* Seeks rational efficiency.	Good as an individual contributor.	38%

crisis by thanking the team publicly for its contribution and appointing new team members. Eventually, in the face of mounting losses arising from this poor management, the board decided to demote the Diplomat to his former role as vice president.

The Expert

The largest category of leader is that of Experts, who account for 38% of all professionals in our sample. In contrast to Opportunists,

Achiever	*Meets strategic goals.* Effectively achieves goals through teams; juggles managerial duties and market demands.	Well suited to managerial roles; action and goal oriented.	30%
Individualist	*Interweaves competing personal and company action logics.* Creates unique structures to resolve gaps between strategy and performance.	Effective in venture and consulting roles.	10%
Strategist	*Generates organizational and personal transforma-tions.* Exercises the power of mutual inquiry, vigilance, and vulnerability for both the short and long term.	Effective as a transfor-mational leader.	4%
Alchemist	*Generates social transformations.* Integrates material, spiritual, and societal transformation.	Good at leading society-wide transformations.	1%

who focus on trying to control the world around them, and Diplomats, who concentrate on controlling their own behavior, Experts try to exercise control by perfecting their knowledge, both in their professional and personal lives. Exercising watertight thinking is extremely important to Experts. Not surprisingly, many accountants, investment analysts, marketing researchers, software engineers, and consultants operate from the Expert action logic. Secure in their expertise, they present hard data and logic in their efforts to gain consensus and buy-in for their proposals.

Experts are great individual contributors because of their pursuit of continuous improvement, efficiency, and perfection. But as managers, they can be problematic because they are so completely sure they are right. When subordinates talk about a my-way-or-the-highway type of boss, they are probably talking about someone operating from an Expert action logic. Experts tend to view collaboration as a waste of time ("Not all meetings are a waste of time—some are canceled!"), and they will frequently treat the opinions of people less expert than themselves with contempt. Emotional intelligence is neither desired nor appreciated. As Sun Microsystems' CEO Scott McNealy put it: "I don't do feelings; I'll leave that to Barry Manilow."

It comes as no surprise, then, that after unsuccessfully pleading with him to scale back in the face of growing losses during the dotcom debacle of 2001 and 2002, nearly a dozen members of McNealy's senior management team left.

The Achiever

For those who hope someday to work for a manager who both challenges and supports them and creates a positive team and interdepartmental atmosphere, the good news is that a large proportion, 30%, of the managers in our research measured as Achievers. While these leaders create a positive work environment and focus their efforts on deliverables, the downside is that their style often inhibits thinking outside the box.

Achievers have a more complex and integrated understanding of the world than do managers who display the three previous action logics we've described. They're open to feedback and realize that many of the ambiguities and conflicts of everyday life are due to differences in interpretation and ways of relating. They know that creatively transforming or resolving clashes requires sensitivity to relationships and the ability to influence others in positive ways. Achievers can also reliably lead a team to implement new strategies over a one- to three-year period, balancing immediate and long-term objectives. One study of ophthalmologists in private practice showed that those who scored as Achievers had lower staff turnover, delegated more responsibility, and had practices that earned at least twice the gross annual revenues of those run by Experts.

Achievers often find themselves clashing with Experts. The Expert subordinate, in particular, finds the Achiever leader hard to take because he cannot deny the reality of the Achiever's success even though he feels superior. Consider Hewlett-Packard, where the research engineers tend to score as Experts and the lab managers as higher-level Achievers. At one project meeting, a lab manager—a decided Achiever—slammed her coffee cup on the table and exclaimed, "I *know* we can get 18 features into this, but the customers want delivery some time this century, and the main eight features will do." "Philistine!" snorted one engineer, an Expert. But this kind of conflict isn't always destructive. In fact, it provides much of the fuel that has ignited—and sustained—the competitiveness of many of the country's most successful corporations.

The Individualist

The Individualist action logic recognizes that neither it nor any of the other action logics are "natural"; all are constructions of oneself and the world. This seemingly abstract idea enables the 10% of Individualist leaders to contribute unique practical value to their organizations; they put personalities and ways of relating into perspective and communicate well with people who have other action logics.

What sets Individualists apart from Achievers is their awareness of a possible conflict between their principles and their actions, or between the organization's values and its implementation of those values. This conflict becomes the source of tension, creativity, and a growing desire for further development.

Individualists also tend to ignore rules they regard as irrelevant, which often makes them a source of irritation to both colleagues and bosses. "So, what do you think?" one of our clients asked us as he was debating whether to let go of one of his star performers, a woman who had been measured as an Individualist. Sharon (not her real name) had been asked to set up an offshore shared service function in the Czech Republic in order to provide IT support to two separate and internally competitive divisions operating there. She formed a highly cohesive team within budget and so far ahead of schedule that she quipped that she was "delivering services before Group Business Risk had delivered its report saying it can't be done."

The trouble was that Sharon had a reputation within the wider organization as a wild card. Although she showed great political savvy when it came to her individual projects, she put many people's noses out of joint in the larger organization because of her unique, unconventional ways of operating. Eventually, the CEO was called in (not for the first time) to resolve a problem created by her failure to acknowledge key organizational processes and people who weren't on her team.

Many of the dynamics created by different action logics are illustrated by this story and its outcome. The CEO, whose own action logic was that of an Achiever, did not see how he could challenge Sharon to develop and move beyond creating such problems. Although ambivalent about her, he decided to retain her because she was delivering and because the organization had recently lost several capable, if unconventional, managers.

So Sharon stayed, but only for a while. Eventually, she left the company to set up an offshoring consultancy. When we examine in the second half of this article how to help executives transform their leadership action logics, we'll return to this story to see how both Sharon and the CEO might have succeeded in transforming theirs.

The Strategist

Strategists account for just 4% of leaders. What sets them apart from Individualists is their focus on organizational constraints and perceptions, which they treat as discussable and transformable. Whereas the Individualist masters communication with colleagues who have different action logics, the Strategist masters the second-order organizational impact of actions and agreements. The Strategist is also adept at creating shared visions across different action logics—visions that encourage both personal and organizational transformations. According to the Strategist's action logic, organizational and social change is an iterative developmental process that requires awareness and close leadership attention.

Strategists deal with conflict more comfortably than do those with other action logics, and they're better at handling people's instinctive resistance to change. As a result, Strategists are highly effective change agents. We found confirmation of this in our recent study of ten CEOs in six different industries. All of their organizations had the stated objective of transforming themselves and had engaged consultants to help with the process. Each CEO filled out a Leadership Development Profile, which showed that five of them were Strategists and the other five fell into other action logics. The Strategists succeeded in generating one or more organizational transformations over a four-year period; their companies' profitability, market share, and reputation all improved. By contrast, only two of the other five CEOs succeeded in transforming their organizations—despite help from consultants, who themselves profiled as Strategists.

Strategists are fascinated with three distinct levels of social interplay: personal relationships, organizational relations, and national and international developments. Consider Joan Bavaria, a CEO who, back in 1985, measured as a Strategist. Bavaria created one of the first socially responsible investment funds, a new subdivision of the investments industry, which by the end of 2001 managed more than $3 trillion in funds. In 1982, Bavaria founded Trillium Asset Management, a worker-owned company, which she still heads. She also cowrote the CERES Environmental Principles, which dozens of major companies have signed. In the late 1990s, CERES, working with the United Nations, created the Global Reporting Initiative, which supports financial, social, and environmental transparency and accountability worldwide.

Here we see the Strategist action logic at work. Bavaria saw a unique moment in which to make ethical investing a viable business, then established Trillium to execute her plan. Strategists typically have socially conscious business ideas that are carried out in a highly collaborative manner. They seek to weave together idealist visions with pragmatic, timely initiatives and principled actions. Bavaria worked beyond the boundaries of her own organization to influence the socially responsible investment industry as a whole and later made the development of social and environmental accountability standards an international endeavor by involving the United Nations. Many Achievers will use their influence to successfully promote their own companies. The Strategist works to create ethical principles and practices beyond the interests of herself or her organization.

The Alchemist

The final leadership action logic for which we have data and experience is the Alchemist. Our studies of the few leaders we have identified as Alchemists suggest that what sets them apart from Strategists is their ability to renew or even reinvent themselves and their organizations in historically significant ways. Whereas the Strategist will move from one engagement to another, the Alchemist has an extraordinary capacity to deal simultaneously with many situations at multiple levels. The Alchemist can talk with both kings and commoners. He can deal with immediate priorities yet never lose sight of long-term goals.

Alchemists constitute 1% of our sample, which indicates how rare it is to find them in business or anywhere else. Through an extensive search process, we found six Alchemists who were willing to participate in an up-close study of their daily actions. Though this is obviously a very small number that cannot statistically justify generalization, it's worth noting that all six Alchemists shared certain characteristics. On a daily basis, all were engaged in multiple organizations and found time to deal with issues raised by each. However, they were not in a constant rush—nor did they devote hours on end to a single activity. Alchemists are typically charismatic and extremely aware individuals who live by high moral standards. They focus intensely on the truth. Perhaps most important, they're able to catch unique moments in the history of their organizations, creating symbols and metaphors that speak to people's hearts and minds. In one conservative financial services company in the UK, a recently appointed CEO turned up for work in a tracksuit instead of his usual pinstripes but said nothing about it to anyone. People wondered whether this was a new dress code. Weeks later, the CEO spoke publicly about his attire and the need to be unconventional and to move with greater agility and speed.

A more celebrated example of an Alchemist is Nelson Mandela. Although we never formally profiled Mandela, he exemplifies the Alchemist action logic. In 1995, Mandela symbolized the unity of a new South Africa when he attended the Rugby World Cup game in which the Springboks, the South African national team, were playing. Rugby had been the bastion of white supremacy, but Mandela attended the game. He walked on to the pitch wearing the Springboks' jersey so hated by black South Africans, at the same time giving the clenched fist salute of the ANC, thereby appealing, almost impossibly, both to black and white South Africans. As Tokyo Sexwale, ANC activist and premier of South Africa's Gauteng province, said of him: "Only Mandela could wear an enemy jersey. Only Mandela would go down there and be associated with the Springboks . . . All the years in the underground, in the trenches, denial, self-denial, away from home, prison, it was worth it. That's all we wanted to see."

Evolving as a Leader

The most remarkable—and encouraging—finding from our research is that leaders can transform from one action logic to another. We have, in fact, documented a number of leaders who have succeeded in transforming themselves from Experts into Achievers, from Achievers into Individualists, and from Individualists into Strategists.

Take the case of Jenny, one of our clients, who initially measured as an Expert. She became disillusioned with her role in her company's PR department and resigned in order to, as she said, "sort out what I really want to do." Six months later, she joined a different company in a similar role, and two years after that we profiled her again and she still measured as an Expert. Her decision to resign from the first company, take a "sabbatical," and then join the second company had made no difference to her action logic. At that point, Jenny chose to join a group of peer leaders committed to examining their current leadership patterns and to experimenting with new ways of acting. This group favored the Strategist perspective (and the founder of the group was profiled as an Alchemist), which in the end helped Jenny's development. She learned that her habit of consistently taking a critical position, which she considered "usefully objective," isolated her and generated distrust. As a result of the peer group's feedback, she started a series of small and private experiments, such as asking questions rather than criticizing. She realized that instead of seeing the faults in others, she had to be clear about what *she* could contribute and, in doing so, started the move from an Expert to an Achiever. Spiritually, Jenny learned that she needed an ongoing community of inquiry at the center of her life and found a spiritual home for continuing reflection in Quaker meetings, which later supported (and indeed signaled) her transition from an Achiever to an Individualist.

Two years later, Jenny left the second job to start her own company, at which point she began profiling as a Strategist. This was a highly unusual movement of three action logics in such a short time. We have had only two other instances in which a leader has transformed twice in less than four years.

As Jenny's case illustrates, there are a number of personal changes that can support leadership transformation. Jenny experienced loss of faith in the system and feelings of boredom, irritability, burnout, depression, and even anger. She began to ask herself existential questions. But another indication of a leader's readiness to transform is an increasing attraction to the qualities she begins to intuit in people with more effective action logics. Jenny, as we saw, was drawn to and benefited hugely from her Strategist peer group as well as from a mentor who exhibited the Alchemist action logic. This search for new perspectives often manifests itself in personal transformations: The ready-to-transform leader starts developing new relationships. She may also explore new forms of spiritual practice or new forms of centering and self-expression, such as playing a musical instrument or doing tai chi.

External events can also trigger and support transformation. A promotion, for example, may give a leader the opportunity to expand his or her range of capabilities. Earlier, we cited the frustration of Expert research engineers at Hewlett-Packard with the product and delivery attitude of Achiever lab managers. Within a year of one engineer's promotion to lab manager, a role that required coordination of others and cooperation across departments, the former Expert was profiling as an Achiever. Although he initially took some heat ("Sellout!") from his former buddies, his new Achiever awareness meant that he was more focused on customers' needs and clearer about delivery schedules. For the first time, he understood the dance between engineers trying to perfect the technology and managers trying to deliver on budget and on schedule.

Changes to a manager's work practices and environment can also facilitate transformation. At one company we studied, leaders changed from Achievers to Individualists partly because of simple organizational and process changes. At the company's senior manager meetings, for example, executives other than the CEO had the chance to lead the meetings; these opportunities, which were supported by new spirit of openness, feedback, and frank debate, fostered professional growth among many of the company's leaders.

Planned and structured development interventions are another means of supporting leadership transformation. We worked with a leading oil and gas exploration company on developing the already high-level capabilities of a pool of future senior managers; the managers were profiled and then interviewed by two consultants who explored each manager's action logic and how it constrained and enabled him or her to perform current and recent roles. Challenges were discussed as well as a view of the individual's potential and a possible developmental plan. After the exercise, several managers, whose Individualist and Strategist capabilities had not been fully understood by the company, were appreciated and engaged differently in their roles. What's more, the organization's own definition of leadership talent was reframed to include the capabilities of the Individualist and Strategist action logics. This in turn demanded that the company radically revisit its competency framework to incorporate such expectations as "sees issues from multiple perspectives" and "creates deep change without formal power."

Now that we've looked generally at some of the changes and interventions that can support leadership development, let's turn to some specifics about how the most common transformations are apt to take place.

From Expert to Achiever

This transformation is the most commonly observed and practiced among businesspeople and by those in management and executive education. For the past generation or more, the training departments of large companies have been supporting the development of managers from Experts into Achievers by running programs with titles like "Management by Objectives," "Effective Delegation," and "Managing People for Results." These programs typically emphasize getting results through flexible strategies rather than through one right method used in one right way.

Observant leaders and executive coaches can also formulate well-structured exercises and questions related to everyday work to help Experts become aware of the different assumptions they and others may be making. These efforts can help Experts practice new conversational strategies such as, "You may be right, but I'd like to understand what leads you to believe that." In addition, those wishing to push Experts to the next level should consider rewarding Achiever competencies like timely delivery of results, the ability to manage for performance, and the ability to implement strategic priorities.

Within business education, MBA programs are apt to encourage the development of the more pragmatic Achievers by frustrating the perfectionist Experts. The heavy workloads, use of multidisciplinary and ambiguous case studies, and teamwork requirements all promote the development of Achievers. By contrast, MSc programs, in particular disciplines such as finance or marketing research, tend to reinforce the Expert perspective.

Still, the transition from Expert to Achiever remains one of the most painful bottlenecks in most organizations. We've all heard the eternal lament of engineers, lawyers, and other professionals whose Expert success has saddled them with managerial duties, only to estrange them from the work they love. Their challenge becomes working as highly effective Achievers who can continue to use their in-depth expertise to succeed as leaders and managers.

From Achiever to Individualist

Although organizations and business schools have been relatively successful in developing leaders to the Achiever action logic, they have, with few exceptions, a dismal record in recognizing, support-ing, and *actively* developing leaders to the Individualist and Strate-gist action logics, let alone to the Alchemist logic. This is not surprising. In many organizations, the Achiever, with his drive and focus on the endgame, is seen as the finish line for development: "This is a competitive industry—we need to keep a sharp focus on the bottom line."

The development of leaders beyond the Achiever action logic requires a very different tack from that necessary to bring about the Expert-to-Achiever transformation. Interventions must encourage self-awareness on the part of the evolving leader as well as a greater awareness of other worldviews. In both business and personal rela-tionships, speaking and listening must come to be experienced not as necessary, taken-for-granted ways of communicating predetermined ideas but as intrinsically forward-thinking, creative actions. Achiev-ers use inquiry to determine whether they (and the teams and organ-ization to which they belong) are accomplishing their goals and how they might accomplish them more effectively. The developing Indi-vidualist, however, begins to inquire about and reflect on the goals themselves—with the aim of improving future goals. Annual devel-opment plans that set new goals, are generated through probing and trusting conversation, are actively supported through executive coaching, and are carefully reviewed at the end of the cycle can be critical enablers at this point. Yet few boards and CEOs appreciate how valuable this time investment can be, and it is all too easily sacrificed in the face of short-term objectives, which can seem more pressing to leaders whose action logics are less developed.

Let's go back to the case of Sharon, the Individualist we described earlier whose Achiever CEO wasn't able to manage her. How might a coach or consultant have helped the CEO feel less threatened by Sharon and more capable of supporting her development while also being more open to his own needs and potential? One way would have been to try role-playing, asking the CEO to play Sharon while the coach or consultant enacts the CEO role. The role-playing might have gone as follows:

"Sharon, I want to talk with you about your future here at our company. Your completion of the Czech project under budget and ahead of time is one more sign that you have the initiative, creativity, and determination to make the senior team here. At the same time, I've had to pick up a number of pieces after you that I shouldn't have had to. I'd like to brainstorm together about how you can approach future projects in a way that eliminates this hassle and gets key players on your side. Then, we can chat several times over the next year as you begin to apply whatever new principles we come up with. Does this seem like a good use of our time, or do you have a different perspective on the issue?"

Note that the consultant in the CEO's role offers clear praise, a clear description of a limitation, a proposed path forward, and an inquiry that empowers the CEO (playing Sharon) to reframe the dilemma if he wishes. Thus, instead of giving the CEO one-way advice about what he should do, the coach enacts a dialogic scenario with him, illustrating a new kind of practice and letting the CEO judge whether the enacted relationship is a positive one. The point is not so much to teach the CEO a new conversational repertoire but to make him more comfortable with how the Individualist sees and makes sense of the world around her and what feedback may motivate her to commit to further learning. Such specific experiments with new ways of listening and talking can gradually dissolve the fears associated with transformational learning.

To Strategist and Beyond

Leaders who are moving toward the Strategist and Alchemist action logics are no longer primarily seeking personal skills that will make them more effective within existing organizational systems. They will already have mastered many of those skills. Rather, they are exploring the disciplines and commitments entailed in creating projects, teams, networks, strategic alliances, and whole organizations on the basis of collaborative inquiry. It is this ongoing practice of reframing inquiry that makes them and their corporations so successful.

The path toward the Strategist and Alchemist action logics is qualitatively different from other leadership development processes. For a start, emergent Strategists and Alchemists are no longer seeking mentors to help them sharpen existing skills and to guide them toward influential networks (although they may seek spiritual and ethical guidance from mentors). Instead, they are seeking to engage in mutual mentoring with peers who are already part of their networks (such as board members, top managers, or leaders within a scientific discipline). The objective of this senior-peer mentoring is not, in conventional terms, to increase the chances of success but to create a sustainable community of people who can challenge the emergent leader's assumptions and practices and those of his company, industry, or other area of activity.

We witnessed just this kind of peer-to-peer development when one senior client became concerned that he, his company, and the industry as a whole were operating at the Achiever level. This concern, of course, was itself a sign of his readiness to transform beyond that logic. This executive—the CEO of a dental hygiene company—and his company were among the most successful of the parent company's subsidiaries. However, realizing that he and those around him had been keeping their heads down, he chose to initiate a research project—on introducing affordable dental hygiene in developing countries—that was decidedly out of the box for him and for the corporation.

The CEO's timing was right for such an initiative, and he used the opportunity to engage in collaborative inquiry with colleagues across the country. Eventually, he proposed an educational and charitable venture, which the parent company funded. The executive was promoted to a new vice presidency for international ventures within the parent company—a role he exercised with an increased sense of collaboration and a greater feeling of social responsibility for his company in emerging markets.

Formal education and development processes can also guide individuals toward a Strategist action logic. Programs in which participants act as leaders and challenge their conventional assumptions about leading and organizing are very effective. Such programs will be either long term (one or two years) or repeated, intense experiences that nurture the moment-to-moment awareness of participants, always providing the shock of dissonance that stimulates them to reexamine their worldviews. Path-breaking programs of this type can be found at a few universities and consultancies around the globe. Bath University in the UK, for instance, sponsors a two-year master's degree in responsibility and business practice in which students work together during six one-week get-togethers. These programs involve small-learning teams, autobiographical writing, psychodrama, deep experiences in nature, and a yearlong business project that involves action and reflection. Interestingly, many people who attend these programs report that these experiences have had the transformative power of a life-altering event, such as a career or existential crisis or a new marriage.

Leadership Teams and Leadership Cultures Within Organizations

So far, our discussion has focused on the leadership styles of individuals. But we have found that our categories of leadership styles can be used to describe teams and organizations as well. Here we will talk briefly about the action logics of teams.

Over the long term, the most effective teams are those with a Strategist culture, in which the group sees business challenges as opportunities for growth and learning on the part of both individuals and the organization. A leadership team at one of the companies we worked with decided to invite managers from across departments to participate in time-to-market new product teams. Seen as a risky distraction, few managers volunteered, except for some Individualists and budding Strategists. However, senior management provided sufficient support and feedback to ensure the teams' early success. Soon, the first participants were promoted and leading their own cross-departmental teams. The Achievers in the organization, seeing that others were being promoted, started volunteering for these teams. Gradually, more people within the organization were experiencing shared leadership, mutual testing of one another's assumptions and practices, and individual challenges that contributed to their development as leaders.

Sadly, few companies use teams in this way. Most senior manager teams operate at the Achiever action logic—they prefer unambiguous targets and deadlines, and working with clear strategies, tactics, and plans, often against tight deadlines. They thrive in a climate of adversity ("When the going gets tough, the tough get going") and derive great pleasure from pulling together and delivering. Typically, the team's leaders and several other members will be Achievers, with several Experts and perhaps one or two Individualists or Strategists (who typically feel ignored). Such Achiever teams are often impatient at slowing down to reflect, are apt to dismiss questions about goals and assumptions as "endless philosophizing," and typically respond with hostile humor to creative exercises, calling them "off-the-wall" diversions. These behaviors will ultimately limit an Achiever team's success.

The situation is worse at large, mature companies where senior management teams operate as Experts. Here, vice presidents see themselves as chiefs and their "teams" as an information-reporting formality. Team life is bereft of shared problem-solving, decision-making, or strategy-formulating efforts. Senior teams limited by the Diplomat action logic are even less functional. They are characterized by strong status differences, undiscussable norms, and ritual "court" ceremonies that are carefully stage-managed.

Individualist teams, which are more likely to be found in creative, consulting, and nonprofit organizations, are relatively rare and very different from Achiever, Expert, and Diplomat teams. In contrast to Achiever teams, they may be strongly reflective; in fact, excessive time may be spent reviewing goals, assumptions, and work practices. Because individual concerns and input are very important to these teams, rapid decision making may be difficult.

But like individual people, teams can change their style. For instance, we've seen Strategist CEOs help Individualist senior teams balance action and inquiry and so transform into Strategist teams. Another example is an Achiever senior team in a financial services company we worked with that was emerging from two years of harsh cost cutting during a market downturn. To adapt to a changing and growing financial services market, the company needed to become significantly more visionary and innovative and learn how to engage its workforce. To lead this transformation, the team had to start with itself. We worked with it to help team members understand the constraints of the Achiever orientation, which required a number of interventions over time. We began by working to improve the way the team discussed issues and by coaching individual members, including the CEO. As the team evolved, it became apparent that its composition needed to change: Two senior executives, who had initially seemed ideally suited to the group because of their achievements, had to be replaced when it became clear that they were unwilling to engage and experiment with the new approach.

During this reorientation, which lasted slightly more than two years, the team became an Individualist group with emergent Strategist capabilities. The CEO, who had profiled at Achiever/Individualist, now profiled as a Strategist, and most other team members showed one developmental move forward. The impact of this was also felt in the team's and organization's ethos: Once functionally divided, the team learned to accept and integrate the diverse opinions of its members. Employee surveys reported increased engagement across the company. Outsiders began seeing the company as ahead of the curve, which meant the organization was better able to attract top talent. In the third year, bottom- and top-line results were well ahead of industry competitors.

The leader's voyage of development is not an easy one. Some people change little in their lifetimes; some change substantially. Despite the undeniably crucial role of genetics, human nature is not fixed. Those who are willing to work at developing themselves and becoming more self-aware can almost certainly evolve over time into truly transformational leaders. Few may become Alchemists, but many will have the desire and potential to become Individualists and Strategists. Corporations that help their executives and leadership teams examine their action logics can reap rich rewards.

Originally published in April 2005. Reprint R0504D

Discovering Your Authentic Leadership

by Bill George, Peter Sims, Andrew N. McLean, and Diana Mayer

DURING THE PAST 50 YEARS, leadership scholars have conducted more than 1,000 studies in an attempt to determine the definitive styles, characteristics, or personality traits of great leaders. None of these studies has produced a clear profile of the ideal leader. Thank goodness. If scholars had produced a cookie-cutter leadership style, individuals would be forever trying to imitate it. They would make themselves into personae, not people, and others would see through them immediately.

No one can be authentic by trying to imitate someone else. You can learn from others' experiences, but there is no way you can be successful when you are trying to be like them. People trust you when you are genuine and authentic, not a replica of someone else. Amgen CEO and president Kevin Sharer, who gained priceless experience working as Jack Welch's assistant in the 1980s, saw the downside of GE's cult of personality in those days. "Everyone wanted to be like Jack," he explains. "Leadership has many voices. You need to be who you are, not try to emulate somebody else."

Over the past five years, people have developed a deep distrust of leaders. It is increasingly evident that we need a new kind of business leader in the twenty-first century. In 2003, Bill George's book, *Authentic Leadership: Rediscovering the Secrets to Creating Lasting Value,* challenged a new generation to lead authentically. Authentic leaders demonstrate a passion for their purpose, practice their values consistently, and lead with their hearts as well as their heads. They establish long-term, meaningful relationships and have the self-discipline to get results. They know who they are.

Many readers of *Authentic Leadership,* including several CEOs, indicated that they had a tremendous desire to become authentic leaders and wanted to know how. As a result, our research team set out to answer the question, "How can people become and remain authentic leaders?" We interviewed 125 leaders to learn how they developed their leadership abilities. These interviews constitute the largest in-depth study of leadership development ever undertaken. Our interviewees discussed openly and honestly how they realized their potential and candidly shared their life stories, personal struggles, failures, and triumphs.

The people we talked with ranged in age from 23 to 93, with no fewer than 15 per decade. They were chosen based on their reputations for authenticity and effectiveness as leaders, as well as our personal knowledge of them. We also solicited recommendations from other leaders and academics. The resulting group includes women and men from a diverse array of racial, religious, and socioeconomic backgrounds and nationalities. Half of them are CEOs, and the other half comprises a range of profit and nonprofit leaders, midcareer leaders, and young leaders just starting on their journeys.

After interviewing these individuals, we believe we understand why more than 1,000 studies have not produced a profile of an ideal leader. Analyzing 3,000 pages of transcripts, our team was startled to see that these people did not identify any universal characteristics, traits, skills, or styles that led to their success. Rather, their leadership emerged from their life stories. Consciously and subconsciously, they were constantly testing themselves through real-world experiences and reframing their life stories to understand who they were at their core. In doing so, they discovered the purpose of their leadership and learned that being authentic made them more effective.

These findings are extremely encouraging: You do not have to be born with specific characteristics or traits of a leader. You do not have to wait for a tap on the shoulder. You do not have to be at the top of your organization. Instead, you can discover your potential right now. As one of our interviewees, Young & Rubicam chairman and CEO Ann Fudge, said, "All of us have the spark of leadership in us, whether it is in business, in government, or as a nonprofit volunteer. The challenge is to understand ourselves well enough to discover where we can use our leadership gifts to serve others."

Discovering your authentic leadership requires a commitment to developing yourself. Like musicians and athletes, you must devote yourself to a lifetime of realizing your potential. Most people Kroger CEO David Dillon has seen become good leaders were self-taught. Dillon said, "The advice I give to individuals in our company is not to expect the company to hand you a development plan. You need to take responsibility for developing yourself."

In the following pages, we draw upon lessons from our interviews to describe how people become authentic leaders. First and most important, they frame their life stories in ways that allow them to see themselves not as passive observers of their lives but rather as individuals who can develop self-awareness from their experiences. Authentic leaders act on that awareness by practicing their values and principles, sometimes at substantial risk to themselves. They are careful to balance their motivations so that they are driven by these inner values as much as by a desire for external rewards or recognition. Authentic leaders also keep a strong support team around them, ensuring that they live integrated, grounded lives.

Learning from Your Life Story

The journey to authentic leadership begins with understanding the story of your life. Your life story provides the context for your experiences, and through it, you can find the inspiration to make an impact in the world. As the novelist John Barth once wrote, "The story of your life is not your life. It is your story." In other words, it is your personal narrative that matters, not the mere facts of your life. Your life narrative is like a permanent recording playing in your head. Over and over, you replay the events and personal interactions that are important to your life, attempting to make sense of them to find your place in the world.

While the life stories of authentic leaders cover the full spectrum of experiences—including the positive impact of parents, athletic coaches, teachers, and mentors—many leaders reported that their motivation came from a difficult experience in their lives. They described the transformative effects of the loss of a job; personal illness; the untimely death of a close friend or relative; and feelings of being excluded, discriminated against, and rejected by peers. Rather than seeing themselves as victims, though, authentic leaders used these formative experiences to give meaning to their lives. They reframed these events to rise above their challenges and to discover their passion to lead.

Let's focus now on one leader in particular, Novartis chairman and CEO Daniel Vasella, whose life story was one of the most difficult of all the people we interviewed. He emerged from extreme challenges in his youth to reach the pinnacle of the global pharmaceutical industry, a trajectory that illustrates the trials many leaders have to go through on their journeys to authentic leadership.

Vasella was born in 1953 to a modest family in Fribourg, Switzerland. His early years were filled with medical problems that stoked his passion to become a physician. His first recollections were of a hospital where he was admitted at age four when he suffered from food poisoning. Falling ill with asthma at age five, he was sent alone to the mountains of eastern Switzerland for two summers. He found the four-month separations from his parents especially difficult because his caretaker had an alcohol problem and was unresponsive to his needs.

At age eight, Vasella had tuberculosis, followed by meningitis, and was sent to a sanatorium for a year. Lonely and homesick, he suffered a great deal that year, as his parents rarely visited him. He still remembers the pain and fear when the nurses held him down during the lumbar punctures so that he would not move. One day, a new physician arrived and took time to explain each step of the procedure.

Vasella asked the doctor if he could hold a nurse's hand rather than being held down. "The amazing thing is that this time the procedure didn't hurt," Vasella recalls. "Afterward, the doctor asked me, 'How was that?' I reached up and gave him a big hug. These human gestures of forgiveness, caring, and compassion made a deep impression on me and on the kind of person I wanted to become."

Throughout his early years, Vasella's life continued to be unsettled. When he was ten, his 18-year-old sister passed away after suffering from cancer for two years. Three years later, his father died in surgery. To support the family, his mother went to work in a distant town and came home only once every three weeks. Left to himself, he and his friends held beer parties and got into frequent fights. This lasted for three years until he met his first girlfriend, whose affection changed his life.

At 20, Vasella entered medical school, later graduating with honors. During medical school, he sought out psychotherapy so he could come to terms with his early experiences and not feel like a victim. Through analysis, he reframed his life story and realized that he wanted to help a wider range of people than he could as an individual practitioner. Upon completion of his residency, he applied to become chief physician at the University of Zurich; however, the search committee considered him too young for the position.

Disappointed but not surprised, Vasella decided to use his abilities to increase his impact on medicine. At that time, he had a growing fascination with finance and business. He talked with the head of the pharmaceutical division of Sandoz, who offered him the opportunity to join the company's U.S. affiliate. In his five years in the United States, Vasella flourished in the stimulating environment, first as a sales representative and later as a product manager, and advanced rapidly through the Sandoz marketing organization.

When Sandoz merged with Ciba-Geigy in 1996, Vasella was named CEO of the combined companies, now called Novartis, despite his young age and limited experience. Once in the CEO's role, Vasella blossomed as a leader. He envisioned the opportunity to build a great global health care company that could help people through lifesaving new drugs, such as Gleevec, which has proved to be highly effective for patients with chronic myeloid leukemia. Drawing on the physician role models of his youth, he built an entirely new Novartis culture centered on compassion, competence, and competition. These moves established Novartis as a giant in the industry and Vasella as a compassionate leader.

Vasella's experience is just one of dozens provided by authentic leaders who traced their inspiration directly from their life stories. Asked what empowered them to lead, these leaders consistently replied that they found their strength through transformative experiences. Those experiences enabled them to understand the deeper purpose of their leadership.

Knowing Your Authentic Self

When the 75 members of Stanford Graduate School of Business's Advisory Council were asked to recommend the most important capability for leaders to develop, their answer was nearly unanimous: self-awareness. Yet many leaders, especially those early in their careers, are trying so hard to establish themselves in the world that they leave little time for self-exploration. They strive to achieve success in tangible ways that are recognized in the external world—money, fame, power, status, or a rising stock price. Often their drive enables them to be professionally successful for a while, but they are unable to sustain that success. As they age, they may find something is missing in their lives and realize they are holding back from being the person they want to be. Knowing their authentic selves requires the courage and honesty to open up and examine their experiences. As they do so, leaders become more humane and willing to be vulnerable.

Of all the leaders we interviewed, David Pottruck, former CEO of Charles Schwab, had one of the most persistent journeys to self-awareness. An all-league football player in high school, Pottruck became MVP of his college team at the University of Pennsylvania. After completing his MBA at Wharton and a stint with Citigroup, he joined Charles Schwab as head of marketing, moving from New York to San Francisco. An extremely hard worker, Pottruck could not understand why his new colleagues resented the long hours he put in and his aggressiveness in pushing for results. "I thought my accomplishments would speak for themselves," he said. "It never occurred to me that my level of energy would intimidate and offend other people, because in my mind I was trying to help the company."

Pottruck was shocked when his boss told him, "Dave, your colleagues do not trust you." As he recalled, "That feedback was like a dagger to my heart. I was in denial, as I didn't see myself as others saw me. I became a lightning rod for friction, but I had no idea how self-serving I looked to other people. Still, somewhere in my inner core the feedback resonated as true." Pottruck realized that he could not succeed unless he identified and overcame his blind spots.

Denial can be the greatest hurdle that leaders face in becoming self-aware. They all have egos that need to be stroked, insecurities that need to be smoothed, fears that need to be allayed. Authentic leaders realize that they have to be willing to listen to feedback— especially the kind they don't want to hear. It was only after his second divorce that Pottruck finally was able to acknowledge that he still had large blind spots: "After my second marriage fell apart, I thought I had a wife-selection problem." Then he worked with a counselor who delivered some hard truths: "The good news is you do not have a wife-selection problem; the bad news is you have a husband-behavior problem." Pottruck then made a determined effort to change. As he described it, "I was like a guy who has had three heart attacks and finally realizes he has to quit smoking and lose some weight."

These days Pottruck is happily remarried and listens carefully when his wife offers constructive feedback. He acknowledges that he falls back on his old habits at times, particularly in high stress situations, but now he has developed ways of coping with stress. "I have had enough success in life to have that foundation of self-respect, so I can take the criticism and not deny it. I have finally learned to tolerate my failures and disappointments and not beat myself up."

Practicing Your Values and Principles

The values that form the basis for authentic leadership are derived from your beliefs and convictions, but you will not know what your true values are until they are tested under pressure. It is relatively easy to list your values and to live by them when things are going well. When your success, your career, or even your life hangs in the balance, you learn what is most important, what you are prepared to sacrifice, and what trade-offs you are willing to make.

Leadership principles are values translated into action. Having a solid base of values and testing them under fire enables you to develop the principles you will use in leading. For example, a value such as "concern for others" might be translated into a leadership principle such as "create a work environment where people are respected for their contributions, provided job security, and allowed to fulfill their potential."

Consider Jon Huntsman, the founder and chairman of Huntsman Corporation. His moral values were deeply challenged when he worked for the Nixon administration in 1972, shortly before Watergate. After a brief stint in the U.S. Department of Health, Education, and Welfare (HEW), he took a job under H.R. Haldeman, President Nixon's powerful chief of staff. Huntsman said he found the experience of taking orders from Haldeman "very mixed. I wasn't geared to take orders, irrespective of whether they were ethically or morally right." He explained, "We had a few clashes, as plenty of things that Haldeman wanted to do were questionable. An amoral atmosphere permeated the White House."

One day, Haldeman directed Huntsman to help him entrap a California congressman who had been opposing a White House initiative. The congressman was part owner of a plant that reportedly employed undocumented workers. To gather information to embarrass the congressman, Haldeman told Huntsman to get the plant manager of a company Huntsman owned to place some undocumented workers at the congressman's plant in an undercover operation.

"There are times when we react too quickly and fail to realize immediately what is right and wrong," Huntsman recalled. "This was one of those times when I didn't think it through. I knew instinctively it was wrong, but it took a few minutes for the notion to percolate. After 15 minutes, my inner moral compass made itself noticed and enabled me to recognize this wasn't the right thing to do. Values that had accompanied me since childhood kicked in. Halfway through my conversation with our plant manager, I said to him, 'Let's not do this. I don't want to play this game. Forget that I called.'"

Huntsman told Haldeman that he would not use his employees in this way. "Here I was saying no to the second most powerful person in the country. He didn't appreciate responses like that, as he viewed them as signs of disloyalty. I might as well have been saying farewell. So be it. I left within the next six months."

Balancing Your Extrinsic and Intrinsic Motivations

Because authentic leaders need to sustain high levels of motivation and keep their lives in balance, it is critically important for them to understand what drives them. There are two types of motivations—extrinsic and intrinsic. Although they are reluctant to admit it, many leaders are propelled to achieve by measuring their success against the outside world's parameters. They enjoy the recognition and status that come with promotions and financial rewards. Intrinsic motivations, on the other hand, are derived from their sense of the meaning of their life. They are closely linked to one's life story and the way one frames it. Examples include personal growth, helping other people develop, taking on social causes, and making a difference in the world. The key is to find a balance between your desires for external validation and the intrinsic motivations that provide fulfillment in your work.

Many interviewees advised aspiring leaders to be wary of getting caught up in social, peer, or parental expectations. Debra Dunn, who has worked in Silicon Valley for decades as a Hewlett-Packard executive, acknowledged the constant pressures from external sources: "The path of accumulating material possessions is clearly laid out. You know how to measure it. If you don't pursue that path, people wonder what is wrong with you. The only way to avoid getting caught up in materialism is to understand where you find happiness and fulfillment."

Moving away from the external validation of personal achievement is not always easy. Achievement-oriented leaders grow so

Your Development as an Authentic Leader

As you read this article, think about the basis for your leadership development and the path you need to follow to become an authentic leader. Then ask yourself these questions:

1. **Which people and experiences in your early life had the greatest impact on you?**

2. **What tools do you use to become self-aware?** What is your authentic self? What are the moments when you say to yourself, this is the real me?

3. **What are your most deeply held values?** Where did they come from? Have your values changed significantly since your childhood? How do your values inform your actions?

4. **What motivates you extrinsically?** What are your intrinsic motivations? How do you balance extrinsic and intrinsic motivation in your life?

5. **What kind of support team do you have?** How can your support team make you a more authentic leader? How should you diversify your team to broaden your perspective?

6. **Is your life integrated?** Are you able to be the same person in all aspects of your life—personal, work, family, and community? If not, what is holding you back?

7. **What does being authentic mean in your life?** Are you more effective as a leader when you behave authentically? Have you ever paid a price for your authenticity as a leader? Was it worth it?

8. **What steps can you take today, tomorrow, and over the next year to develop your authentic leadership?**

---

accustomed to successive accomplishments throughout their early years that it takes courage to pursue their intrinsic motivations. But at some point, most leaders recognize that they need to address more difficult questions in order to pursue truly meaningful success. McKinsey's Alice Woodwark, who at 29 has already achieved notable success, reflected: "My version of achievement was pretty naive, born of things I learned early in life about praise and being valued. But if you're just chasing the rabbit around the course, you're not running toward anything meaningful."

Intrinsic motivations are congruent with your values and are more fulfilling than extrinsic motivations. John Thain, CEO of the New York Stock Exchange, said, "I am motivated by doing a really good job at whatever I am doing, but I prefer to multiply my impact on society through a group of people." Or as Ann Moore, chairman and CEO of Time, put it, "I came here 25 years ago solely because I loved magazines and the publishing world." Moore had a dozen job offers after business school but took the lowest-paying one with Time because of her passion for publishing.

Building Your Support Team

Leaders cannot succeed on their own; even the most outwardly confident executives need support and advice. Without strong relationships to provide perspective, it is very easy to lose your way.

Authentic leaders build extraordinary support teams to help them stay on course. Those teams counsel them in times of uncertainty, help them in times of difficulty, and celebrate with them in times of success. After their hardest days, leaders find comfort in being with people on whom they can rely so they can be open and vulnerable. During the low points, they cherish the friends who appreciate them for who they are, not what they are. Authentic leaders find that their support teams provide affirmation, advice, perspective, and calls for course corrections when needed.

How do you go about building your support team? Most authentic leaders have a multifaceted support structure that includes their spouses or significant others, families, mentors, close friends, and colleagues. They build their networks over time, as the experiences, shared histories, and openness with people close to them create the trust and confidence they need in times of trial and uncertainty. Leaders must give as much to their supporters as they get from them so that mutually beneficial relationships can develop.

It starts with having at least one person in your life with whom you can be completely yourself, warts and all, and still be accepted unconditionally. Often that person is the only one who can tell you the honest truth. Most leaders have their closest relationships with their spouses, although some develop these bonds with another family member, a close friend, or a trusted mentor. When leaders can rely on unconditional support, they are more likely to accept themselves for who they really are.

Many relationships grow over time through an expression of shared values and a common purpose. Randy Komisar of venture capital firm Kleiner Perkins Caufield & Byers said his marriage to Hewlett-Packard's Debra Dunn is lasting because it is rooted in similar values. "Debra and I are very independent but extremely harmonious in terms of our personal aspirations, values, and principles. We have a strong resonance around questions like, 'What is your legacy in this world?' It is important to be in sync about what we do with our lives."

Many leaders have had a mentor who changed their lives. The best mentoring interactions spark mutual learning, exploration of similar values, and shared enjoyment. If people are only looking for a leg up from their mentors, instead of being interested in their mentors' lives as well, the relationships will not last for long. It is the two-way nature of the connection that sustains it.

Personal and professional support groups can take many forms. Piper Jaffray's Tad Piper is a member of an Alcoholics Anonymous group. He noted, "These are not CEOs. They are just a group of nice, hard-working people who are trying to stay sober, lead good lives, and work with each other about being open, honest, and vulnerable. We reinforce each other's behavior by talking about our chemical dependency in a disciplined way as we go through the 12 steps. I feel blessed to be surrounded by people who are thinking about those kinds of issues and actually doing something, not just talking about them."

Bill George's experiences echo Piper's: In 1974, he joined a men's group that formed after a weekend retreat. More than 30 years later, the group is still meeting every Wednesday morning. After an opening period of catching up on each other's lives and dealing with any particular difficulty someone may be facing, one of the group's eight members leads a discussion on a topic he has selected. These discussions are open, probing, and often profound. The key to their success is that people say what they really believe without fear of judgment, criticism, or reprisal. All the members consider the group to be one of the most important aspects of their lives, enabling them to clarify their beliefs, values, and understanding of vital issues, as well as serving as a source of honest feedback when they need it most.

Integrating Your Life by Staying Grounded

Integrating their lives is one of the greatest challenges leaders face. To lead a balanced life, you need to bring together all of its constituent elements—work, family, community, and friends—so that you can be the same person in each environment. Think of your life as a house, with a bedroom for your personal life, a study for your professional life, a family room for your family, and a living room to share with your friends. Can you knock down the walls between these rooms and be the same person in each of them?

As John Donahoe, president of eBay Marketplaces and former worldwide managing director of Bain, stressed, being authentic means maintaining a sense of self no matter where you are. He warned, "The world can shape you if you let it. To have a sense of yourself as you live, you must make conscious choices. Sometimes the choices are really hard, and you make a lot of mistakes."

Authentic leaders have a steady and confident presence. They do not show up as one person one day and another person the next. Integration takes discipline, particularly during stressful times when it is easy to become reactive and slip back into bad habits. Donahoe feels strongly that integrating his life has enabled him to become a more effective leader. "There is no nirvana," he said. "The struggle is constant, as the trade-offs don't get any easier as you get older." But for authentic leaders, personal and professional lives are not a zero-sum game. As Donahoe said, "I have no doubt today that my children have made me a far more effective leader in the workplace. Having a strong personal life has made the difference."

Leading is high-stress work. There is no way to avoid stress when you are responsible for people, organizations, outcomes, and managing the constant uncertainties of the environment. The higher you go, the greater your freedom to control your destiny but also the higher the degree of stress. The question is not whether you can avoid stress but how you can control it to maintain your own sense of equilibrium.

Authentic leaders are constantly aware of the importance of staying grounded. Besides spending time with their families and close friends, authentic leaders get physical exercise, engage in spiritual practices, do community service, and return to the places where they grew up. All are essential to their effectiveness as leaders, enabling them to sustain their authenticity.

Empowering People to Lead

Now that we have discussed the process of discovering your authentic leadership, let's look at how authentic leaders empower people in their organizations to achieve superior long-term results, which is the bottom line for all leaders.

Authentic leaders recognize that leadership is not about their success or about getting loyal subordinates to follow them. They know the key to a successful organization is having empowered leaders at all levels, including those who have no direct reports. They not only inspire those around them, they empower those individuals to step up and lead.

A reputation for building relationships and empowering people was instrumental in chairman and CEO Anne Mulcahy's stunning turnaround of Xerox. When Mulcahy was asked to take the company's reins from her failed predecessor, Xerox had $18 billion in debt, and all credit lines were exhausted. With the share price in free fall, morale was at an all-time low. To make matters worse, the SEC was investigating the company's revenue recognition practices.

Mulcahy's appointment came as a surprise to everyone—including Mulcahy herself. A Xerox veteran, she had worked in field sales and on the corporate staff for 25 years, but not in finance, R&D, or manufacturing. How could Mulcahy cope with this crisis when she had had no financial experience? She brought to the CEO role the relationships she had built over 25 years, an impeccable understanding of the organization, and, above all, her credibility as an authentic leader. She bled for Xerox, and everyone knew it. Because of that, they were willing to go the extra mile for her.

After her appointment, Mulcahy met personally with the company's top 100 executives to ask them if they would stay with the company despite the challenges ahead. "I knew there were people-who weren't supportive of me," she said. "So I confronted a couple of them and said, 'This is about the company.'" The first two people Mulcahy talked with, both of whom ran big operating units, decided to leave, but the remaining 98 committed to stay.

Throughout the crisis, people in Xerox were empowered by Mulcahy to step up and lead in order to restore the company to its former greatness. In the end, her leadership enabled Xerox to avoid bankruptcy as she paid back $10 billion in debt and restored revenue growth and profitability with a combination of cost savings and innovative new products. The stock price tripled as a result.

Like Mulcahy, all leaders have to deliver bottom-line results. By creating a virtuous circle in which the results reinforce the effectiveness of their leadership, authentic leaders are able to sustain those results through good times and bad. Their success enables them to attract talented people and align employees' activities with shared goals, as they empower others on their team to lead by taking on greater challenges. Indeed, superior results over a sustained period of time are the ultimate mark of an authentic leader. It may be possible to drive short-term outcomes without being authentic, but authentic leadership is the only way we know to create sustainable long-term results.

For authentic leaders, there are special rewards. No individual achievement can equal the pleasure of leading a group of people to achieve a worthy goal. When you cross the finish line together, all the pain and suffering you may have experienced quickly vanishes. It is replaced by a deep inner satisfaction that you have empowered others and thus made the world a better place. That's the challenge and the fulfillment of authentic leadership.

Originally published in February 2007. Reprint R0702H

In Praise of the Incomplete Leader

by Deborah Ancona, Thomas W. Malone,
Wanda J. Orlikowski, and Peter M. Senge

WE'VE COME TO EXPECT A LOT OF OUR LEADERS. Top executives, the thinking goes, should have the intellectual capacity to make sense of unfathomably complex issues, the imaginative powers to paint a vision of the future that generates everyone's enthusiasm, the operational know-how to translate strategy into concrete plans, and the interpersonal skills to foster commitment to undertakings that could cost people's jobs should they fail. Unfortunately, no single person can possibly live up to those standards.

It's time to end the myth of the complete leader: the flawless person at the top who's got it all figured out. In fact, the sooner leaders stop trying to be all things to all people, the better off their organizations will be. In today's world, the executive's job is no longer to command and control but to cultivate and coordinate the actions of others at all levels of the organization. Only when leaders come to see themselves as incomplete—as having both strengths and weaknesses—will they be able to make up for their missing skills by relying on others.

Corporations have been becoming less hierarchical and more collaborative for decades, of course, as globalization and the growing importance of knowledge work have required that responsibility and initiative be distributed more widely. Moreover, it is now possible for large groups of people to coordinate their actions, not just by bringing lots of information to a few centralized places but also by bringing lots of information to lots of places through ever-growing networks within and beyond the firm. The sheer complexity and ambiguity of problems is humbling. More and more decisions are made in the context of global markets and rapidly—sometimes radically—changing financial, social, political, techno-logical, and environmental forces. Stakeholders such as activists, regulators, and employees all have claims on organizations.

No one person could possibly stay on top of everything. But the myth of the complete leader (and the attendant fear of appearing in-competent) makes many executives try to do just that, exhausting themselves and damaging their organizations in the process. The in-complete leader, by contrast, knows when to let go: when to let those who know the local market do the advertising plan or when to let the engineering team run with its idea of what the customer needs. The incomplete leader also knows that leadership exists throughout the organizational hierarchy—wherever expertise, vision, new ideas, and commitment are found.

We've worked with hundreds of people who have struggled under the weight of the myth of the complete leader. Over the past six years, our work at the MIT Leadership Center has included study-ing leadership in many organizations and teaching the topic to sen-ior executives, middle managers, and MBA students. In our practice-based programs, we have analyzed numerous accounts of organizational change and watched leaders struggle to meld top-down strategic initiatives with vibrant ideas from the rest of the organization.

All this work has led us to develop a model of distributed leader-ship. This framework, which synthesizes our own research with ideas from other leadership scholars, views leadership as a set of four capabilities: *sensemaking* (understanding the context in which a company and its people operate), *relating* (building relationships within and across organizations), *visioning* (creating a compelling picture of the future), and *inventing* (developing new ways to achieve the vision).

Idea in Brief

Have you ever feigned confidence to superiors or reports? Hidden the fact you were confused by the latest business results or blindsided by a competitor's move? If so, you've bought into the **myth of the complete leader:** the flawless being at the top who's got it all figured out.

It's an alluring myth. But in today's world of increasingly complex problems, no human being can meet this standard. Leaders who try only exhaust themselves, endangering their organizations.

Ancona and her coauthors suggest a better way to lead: Accept that you're human, with strengths and weaknesses. Understand the four leadership capabilities all organizations need:

- Sensemaking—interpreting developments in the business environment

- Relating—building trusting relationships

- Visioning—communicating a compelling image of the future

- Inventing—coming up with new ways of doing things

Then find and work with others who can provide the capabilities you're missing.

Take this approach, and you promote leadership throughout your organization, unleashing the expertise, vision, and new ideas your company needs to excel.

While somewhat simplified, these capabilities span the intellectual and interpersonal, the rational and intuitive, and the conceptual and creative capacities required in today's business environment. Rarely, if ever, will someone be equally skilled in all four domains. Thus, incomplete leaders differ from incompetent leaders in that they understand what they're good at and what they're not and have good judgment about how they can work with others to build on their strengths and offset their limitations.

Sometimes, leaders need to further develop the capabilities they are weakest in. The exhibits throughout this article provide some suggestions for when and how to do that. Other times, however, it's more important for leaders to find and work with others to compensate for their weaknesses. Teams and organizations—not just individuals—can use this framework to diagnose their strengths and weaknesses and find ways to balance their skill sets.

Idea in Practice

Incomplete leaders find people throughout their company who can complement their strengths and offset their weaknesses. To do this, understand the four leadership capabilities organizations need. Then diagnose your strength in each:

Capability	What it means	Example	Look for help in this capability if you ...
Sensemaking	Constantly understanding changes in the business environment and interpreting their ramifications for your industry and company	A CEO asks, "How will new technologies reshape our industry?" "How does globalization of labor markets affect our recruitment strategy?"	• Feel strongly that you're always right. • Frequently get blindsided by changes in your company or industry. • Feel resentful when things change.
Relating	Building trusting relationships, balancing advocacy (explaining your viewpoints) with inquiry (listening to understand others' viewpoints), and cultivating networks of supportive confidants	Former Southwest Airlines CEO Herb Kelleher excels at building trusting relationships. He wasn't afraid to tell employees he loved them, and reinforced those emotional bonds with equitable compensation and profit sharing.	• Blame others for failed projects. • Feel others are constantly letting you down or that they can't be trusted. • Frequently experience unpleasant, frustrating, or argumentative interactions with others.

Sensemaking

The term "sensemaking" was coined by organizational psychologist Karl Weick, and it means just what it sounds like: making sense of the world around us. Leaders are constantly trying to understand the contexts they are operating in. How will new technologies reshape the industry? How will changing cultural expectations shift the role of business in society? How does the globalization of labor markets affect recruitment and expansion plans?

Visioning	Creating credible and compelling images of a desired future that people in the organization want to create together	eBay founder Pierre Omidyar envisioned a new way of doing large-scale retailing: an online community where users took responsibility for what happened and had equal access to information.	• Often wonder, "Why are we doing this?" or "Does it really matter?" • Can't remember the last time you felt excited about your work. • Feel you're lacking sense of larger purpose.
Inventing	Creating new ways of approaching tasks or overcoming seemingly insurmountable problems to turn visions into reality	eBay CEO Meg Whitman helped bring Omidyar's vision of online retailing to life by inventing ways to deal with security, vendor reliability, and product diversification.	• Have difficulty relating the company's vision to what you're doing today. • Notice gaps between your firm's aspirations and the way work is organized. • Find that things tend to revert to business as usual.

Weick likened the process of sensemaking to cartography. What we map depends on where we look, what factors we choose to focus on, and what aspects of the terrain we decide to represent. Since these choices will shape the kind of map we produce, there is no perfect map of a terrain. Therefore, making sense is more than an act of analysis; it's an act of creativity. (See the exhibit "Engage in Sensemaking.")

The key for leaders is to determine what would be a useful map given their particular goals and then to draw one that adequately

Engage in sensemaking

1. Get data from multiple sources: customers, suppliers, employees, competitors, other departments, and investors.

2. Involve others in your sensemaking. Say what you think you are seeing, and check with people who have different perspectives from yours.

3. Use early observations to shape small experiments in order to test your conclusions. Look for new ways to articulate alternatives and better ways to understand options.

4. Do not simply apply existing frameworks but instead be open to new possibilities. Try not to describe the world in stereotypical ways, such as good guys and bad guys, victims and oppressors, or marketers and engineers.

represents the situation the organization is facing at that moment. Executives who are strong in this capability know how to quickly capture the complexities of their environment and explain them to others in simple terms. This helps ensure that everyone is working from the same map, which makes it far easier to discuss and plan for the journey ahead. Leaders need to have the courage to present a map that highlights features they believe to be critical, even if their map doesn't conform to the dominant perspective.

When John Reed was CEO of Citibank, the company found itself in a real estate crisis. At the time, common wisdom said that Citibank would need to take a $2 billion write-off, but Reed wasn't sure. He wanted a better understanding of the situation, so to map the problem, he met with federal regulators as well as his managers, the board, potential investors, economists, and real estate experts. He kept asking, "What am I missing here?" After those meetings, he had a much stronger grasp of the problem, and he recalibrated the write-off to $5 billion—which turned out to be a far more accurate estimate. Later, three quarters into the bank's eight-quarter program to deal with the crisis, Reed realized that progress had stopped. He began talking to other CEOs known for their change management skills. This informal benchmarking process led him to devise an organizational redesign.

Throughout the crisis, real estate valuations, investors' requirements, board demands, and management team expectations were all changing and constantly needed to be reassessed. Good leaders understand that sensemaking is a continuous process; they let the map emerge from a melding of observations, data, experiences, conversations, and analyses. In healthy organizations, this sort of sensemaking goes on all the time. People have ongoing dialogues about their interpretations of markets and organizational realities.

At IDEO, a product design firm, sensemaking is step one for all design teams. According to founder David Kelley, team members must act as anthropologists studying an alien culture to understand the potential product from all points of view. When brainstorming a new design, IDEO's teams consider multiple perspectives—that is, they build multiple maps to inform their creative process. One IDEO team was charged with creating a new design for an emergency room. To better understand the experience of a key stakeholder—the patient—team members attached a camera to a patient's head and captured his experience in the ER. The result: nearly ten full hours of film of the ceiling. The sensemaking provoked by this perspective led to a redesign of the ceiling that made it more aesthetically pleasing and able to display important information for patients.

Relating

Many executives who attempt to foster trust, optimism, and consensus often reap anger, cynicism, and conflict instead. That's because they have difficulty relating to others, especially those who don't make sense of the world the way they do. Traditional images of leadership didn't assign much value to relating. Flawless leaders shouldn't need to seek counsel from anyone outside their tight inner circle, the thinking went, and they were expected to issue edicts rather than connect on an emotional level. Times have changed, of course, and in this era of networks, being able to build trusting relationships is a requirement of effective leadership.

Three key ways to do this are *inquiring, advocating,* and *connecting.* The concepts of inquiring and advocating stem from the work of organizational development specialists Chris Argyris and Don Schon. Inquiring means listening with the intention of genuinely understanding the thoughts and feelings of the speaker. Here, the listener suspends judgment and tries to comprehend how and why the speaker has moved from the data of his or her experiences to particular interpretations and conclusions.

Advocating, as the term implies, means explaining one's own point of view. It is the flip side of inquiring, and it's how leaders make clear to others how they reached their interpretations and conclusions. Good leaders distinguish their observations from their opinions and judgments and explain their reasoning without aggression or defensiveness. People with strong relating skills are typically those who've found a healthy balance between inquiring and advocating: They actively try to understand others' views but are able to stand up for their own. (See the exhibit "Build Relationships.")

We've seen countless relationships undermined because people disproportionately emphasized advocating over inquiring. Even though managers pay lip service to the importance of mutual understanding and shared commitment to a course of action, often their real focus is on winning the argument rather than strengthening the connection. Worse, in many organizations, the imbalance goes so far that having one's point of view prevail is what is understood as leadership.

Effective relating does not mean avoiding interpersonal conflict altogether. Argyris and Schon found that "maintaining a smooth

Build relationships

1. Spend time trying to understand others' perspectives, listening with an open mind and without judgment.

2. Encourage others to voice their opinions. What do they care about? How do they interpret what's going on? Why?

3. Before expressing your ideas, try to anticipate how others will react to them and how you might best explain them.

4. When expressing your ideas, don't just give a bottom line; explain your reasoning process.

5. Assess the strengths of your current connections: How well do you relate to others when receiving advice? When giving advice? When thinking through difficult problems? When asking for help?

surface" of conviviality and apparent agreement is one of the most common defensive routines that limits team effectiveness. Balancing inquiring and advocating is ultimately about showing respect, challenging opinions, asking tough questions, and taking a stand.

Consider Twynstra Gudde (TG), one of the largest independent consulting companies in the Netherlands. A few years ago, it replaced the role of CEO with a team of four managing directors who share leadership responsibilities. Given this unique structure, it's vital that these directors effectively relate to one another. They've adopted simple rules, such as a requirement that each leader give his opinion on every issue, majority-rules voting, and veto power for each director.

Clearly, for TG's senior team model to work, members must be skilled at engaging in dialogue together. They continually practice both inquiring and advocating, and because each director can veto a decision, each must thoroughly explain his reasoning to convince the others' that his perspective has merit. It's not easy to reach this level of mutual respect and trust, but over time, the team members' willingness to create honest connections with one another has paid off handsomely. Although they don't always reach consensus, they are able to settle on a course of action. Since this new form of leadership was introduced, TG has thrived: The company's profits have doubled, and employee satisfaction levels have improved. What's more, TG's leadership structure has served as a model for cooperation throughout the organization as well as in the firm's relations with its clients.

The third aspect of relating, connecting, involves cultivating a network of confidants who can help a leader accomplish a wide range of goals. Leaders who are strong in this capability have many people they can turn to who can help them think through difficult problems or support them in their initiatives. They understand that the time spent building and maintaining these connections is time spent investing in their leadership skills. Because no one person can possibly have all the answers, or indeed, know all the right questions to ask, it's crucial that leaders be able to tap into a network of people who can fill in the gaps.

Visioning

Sensemaking and relating can be called the enabling capabilities of leadership. They help set the conditions that motivate and sustain change. The next two leadership capabilities—what we call "visioning" and inventing—are creative and action oriented: They produce the focus and energy needed to make change happen.

Visioning involves creating compelling images of the future. While sensemaking charts a map of what is, visioning produces a map of what could be and, more important, what a leader wants the future to be. It consists of far more than pinning a vision statement to the wall. Indeed, a shared vision is not a static thing—it's an ongoing process. Like sensemaking, visioning is dynamic and collaborative, a process of articulating what the members of an organization want to create together.

Fundamentally, visioning gives people a sense of meaning in their work. Leaders who are skilled in this capability are able to get people excited about their view of the future while inviting others to help crystallize that image. (See the exhibit "Create a Vision.") If they realize other people aren't joining in or buying into the vision, they don't just turn up the volume; they engage in a dialogue about the reality they hope to produce. They use stories and metaphors to paint a vivid picture of what the vision will accomplish, even if they don't have a comprehensive plan for getting there. They know that if the vision is credible and compelling enough, others will generate ideas to advance it.

In South Africa in the early 1990s, a joke was making the rounds: Given the country's daunting challenges, people had two options, one practical and the other miraculous. The practical option was for everyone to pray for a band of angels to come down from heaven and fix things. The miraculous option was for people to talk with one another until they could find a way forward. In F.W. de Klerk's famous speech in 1990—his first after assuming leadership—he called for a nonracist South Africa and suggested that negotiation was the only way to achieve a peaceful transition. That speech sparked a set of changes that led to Nelson Mandela's release from Robben Island

---

Create a vision

1. Practice creating a vision in many arenas, including your work life, your home life, and in community groups. Ask yourself, "What do I want to create?"

2. Develop a vision about something that inspires you. Your enthusiasm will motivate you and others. Listen to what they find exciting and important.

3. Expect that not all people will share your passion. Be prepared to explain why people should care about your vision and what can be achieved through it. If people don't get it, don't just turn up the volume. Try to construct a shared vision.

4. Don't worry if you don't know how to accomplish the vision. If it is compelling and credible, other people will discover all sorts of ways to make it real—ways you never could have imagined on your own.

5. Use images, metaphors, and stories to convey complex situations that will enable others to act.

---

prison and the return to the country of previously banned political leaders.

Few of South Africa's leaders agreed on much of anything regarding the country's future. It seemed like a long shot, at best, that a scenario-planning process convened by a black professor from the University of the Western Cape and facilitated by a white Canadian from Royal Dutch Shell would be able to bring about any sort of change. But they, together with members of the African National Congress (ANC), the radical Pan Africanist Congress (PAC), and the white business community, were charged with forging a new path for South Africa.

When the team members first met, they focused on collective sensemaking. Their discussions then evolved into a yearlong visioning process. In his book, *Solving Tough Problems,* Adam Kahane, the facilitator, says the group started by telling stories of "left-wing revolution, right-wing revolts, and free market utopias." Eventually, the leadership team drafted a set of scenarios that described the many paths toward disaster and the one toward sustainable development.

They used metaphors and clear imagery to convey the various paths in language that was easy to understand. One negative scenario, for instance, was dubbed "Ostrich": A nonrepresentative white government sticks its head in the sand, trying to avoid a negotiated settlement with the black majority. Another negative scenario was labeled "Icarus": A constitutionally unconstrained black government comes to power with noble intentions and embarks on a huge, unsustainable public-spending spree that crashes the economy. This scenario contradicted the popular belief that the country was rich and could simply redistribute wealth from whites to blacks. The Icarus scenario set the stage for a fundamental (and controversial) shift in economic thinking in the ANC and other left-wing parties—a shift that led the ANC government to "strict and consistent fiscal discipline," according to Kahane.

The group's one positive scenario involved the government adopting a set of sustainable policies that would put the country on a path of inclusive growth to successfully rebuild the economy and establish democracy. This option was called "Flamingo," invoking the image of a flock of beautiful birds all taking flight together.

This process of visioning unearthed an extraordinary collective sense of possibility in South Africa. Instead of talking about what other people should do to advance some agenda, the leaders spoke about what they could do to create a better future for everyone. They didn't have an exact implementation plan at the ready, but by creating a credible vision, they paved the way for others to join in and help make their vision a reality.

Leaders who excel in visioning walk the walk; they work to embody the core values and ideas contained in the vision. Darcy Winslow, Nike's global director for women's footwear, is a good example. A 14-year veteran at Nike, Winslow previously held the position of general manager of sustainable business opportunities at the shoe and apparel giant. Her work in that role reflected her own core values, including her passion for the environment. "We had come to see that our customers' health and our own ability to compete were inseparable from the health of the environment," she says. So she initiated the concept of ecologically intelligent product design. Winslow's team worked at determining the chemical composition and environmental effects of every material and process Nike used. They visited factories in China and collected samples of rubber, leather, nylon, polyester, and foams to determine their chemical makeup. This led Winslow and her team to develop a list of "positive" materials—those that weren't harmful to the environment—that they hoped to use in more Nike products. "Environmental sustainability" was no longer just an abstract term on a vision statement; the team now felt a mandate to realize the vision.

Inventing

Even the most compelling vision will lose its power if it floats, unconnected, above the everyday reality of organizational life. To transform a vision of the future into a present-day reality, leaders need to devise processes that will give it life. This inventing is what moves a business from the abstract world of ideas to the concrete world of implementation. In fact, inventing is similar to execution, but the label "inventing" emphasizes that this process often requires creativity to help people figure out new ways of working together.

To realize a new vision, people usually can't keep doing the same things they've been doing. They need to conceive, design, and put into practice new ways of interacting and organizing. Some of the most famous examples of large-scale organizational innovation come from the automotive industry: Henry Ford's conception of the assembly-line factory and Toyota's famed integrated production system.

More recently, Pierre Omidyar, the founder of eBay, invented through his company a new way of doing large-scale retailing. His vision was of an online community where users would take responsibility for what happened. In a 2001 BusinessWeek Online interview, Omidyar explained, "I had the idea that I wanted to create an efficient market and a level playing field where everyone had equal access to information. I wanted to give the power of the market back to individuals, not just large corporations. That was the driving motivation for creating eBay at the start."

Consequently, eBay outsources most of the functions of traditional retailing—purchasing, order fulfillment, and customer service, for example—to independent sellers worldwide. The company estimates that more than 430,000 people make their primary living from selling wares on eBay. If those individuals were all employees of eBay, it would be the second largest private employer in the United States after Wal-Mart.

The people who work through eBay are essentially independent store owners, and, as such, they have a huge amount of autonomy in how they do their work. They decide what to sell, when to sell it, how to price, and how to advertise. Coupled with this individual freedom is global scale. EBay's infrastructure enables them to sell their goods all over the world. What makes eBay's inventing so radical is that it represents a new relationship between an organization and its parts. Unlike typical outsourcing, eBay doesn't pay its retailers—they pay the company.

Inventing doesn't have to occur on such a grand scale. It happens every time a person creates a way of approaching a task or figures out how to overcome a previously insurmountable obstacle. In their book *Car Launch,* George Roth and Art Kleiner describe a highly successful product development team in the automobile industry that struggled with completing its designs on time. Much of the source of the problem, the team members concluded, came from the stovepipe organizational structure found in the product development division. Even though they were a "colocated" team dedicated to designing a common new car, members were divided by their different technical expertise, experience, jargon, and norms of working.

When the team invented a mechanical prototyping device that complemented its computer-aided design tools, the group members found that it facilitated a whole new way of collaborating. Multiple groups within the team could quickly create physical mock-ups of design ideas to be tested by the various engineers from different specialties in the team. The group called the device "the harmony buck," because it helped people break out of their comfortable engineering specialties and solve interdependent design problems together. Development of a "full body" physical mock-up of the new car allowed engineers to hang around the prototype, providing a central focal point for their interactions. It enabled them to more easily identify and raise cross-functional issues, and it facilitated mutual problem solving and coordination.

Cultivate inventiveness

1. Don't assume that the way things have always been done is the best way to do them.

2. When a new task or change effort emerges, encourage creative ways of getting it done.

3. Experiment with different ways of organizing work. Find alternative methods for grouping and linking people.

4. When working to understand your current environment, ask yourself, "What other options are possible?"

In sum, leaders must be able to succeed at inventing, and this requires both attention to detail and creativity. (See the exhibit "Cultivate Inventiveness.")

Balancing the Four Capabilities

Sensemaking, relating, visioning, and inventing are interdependent. Without sensemaking, there's no common view of reality from which to start. Without relating, people work in isolation or, worse, strive toward different aims. Without visioning, there's no shared direction. And without inventing, a vision remains illusory. No one leader, however, will excel at all four capabilities in equal measure.

Typically, leaders are strong in one or two capabilities. Intel chairman Andy Grove is the quintessential sensemaker, for instance, with a gift for recognizing strategic inflection points that can be exploited for competitive advantage. Herb Kelleher, the former CEO of Southwest Airlines, excels at relating. He remarked in the journal *Leader to Leader* that "We are not afraid to talk to our people with emotion. We're not afraid to tell them, 'We love you.' Because we do." With this emotional connection comes equitable compensation and profit sharing.

Apple CEO Steve Jobs is a visionary whose ambitious dreams and persuasiveness have catalyzed remarkable successes for Apple, Next, and Pixar. Meg Whitman, the CEO of eBay, helped bring Pierre Omidyar's vision of online retailing to life by inventing ways to deal with security, vendor reliability, and product diversification.

Once leaders diagnose their own capabilities, identifying their unique set of strengths and weaknesses, they must search for others

Examining Your Leadership Capabilities

Few people wake up in the morning and say, "I'm a poor sensemaker" or "I just can't relate to others." They tend to experience their own weaknesses more as chronic or inexplicable failures in the organization or in those around them. The following descriptions will help you recognize opportunities to develop your leadership capabilities and identify openings for working with others.

Signs of Weak Sensemaking

1. You feel strongly that you are usually right and others are often wrong.

2. You feel your views describe reality correctly, but others' views do not.

3. You find you are often blindsided by changes in your organization or industry.

4. When things change, you typically feel resentful. (That's not the way it should be!)

Signs of Weak Relating

1. You blame others for failed projects.

2. You feel others are constantly letting you down or failing to live up to your expectations.

---

who can provide the things they're missing. (See the sidebar "Examining Your Leadership Capabilities.") Leaders who choose only people who mirror themselves are likely to find their organizations tilting in one direction, missing one or more essential capabilities needed to survive in a changing, complex world. That's why it's important to examine the whole organization to make sure it is appropriately balanced as well. It's the leader's responsibility to create an environment that lets people complement one another's strengths and offset one another's weaknesses. In this way, leadership is distributed across multiple people throughout the organization.

Years ago, one of us attended a three-day meeting on leadership with 15 top managers from different companies. At the close of it,

3. You find that many of your interactions at work are unpleasant, frustrating, or argumentative.

4. You find many of the people you work with untrustworthy.

Signs of Weak Visioning

1. You feel your work involves managing an endless series of crises.

2. You feel like you're bouncing from pillar to post with no sense of larger purpose.

3. You often wonder, "Why are we doing this?" or "Does it really matter?"

4. You can't remember the last time you talked to your family or a friend with excitement about your work.

Signs of Weak Inventing

1. Your organization's vision seems abstract to you.

2. You have difficulty relating your company's vision to what you are doing today.

3. You notice dysfunctional gaps between your organization's aspirations and the way work is organized.

4. You find that things tend to revert to business as usual.

participants were asked to reflect on their experience as leaders. One executive, responsible for more than 50,000 people in his division of a manufacturing corporation, drew two pictures on a flip chart. The image on the left was what he projected to the outside world: It was a large, intimidating face holding up a huge fist. The image on the right represented how he saw himself: a small face with wide eyes, hair standing on end, and an expression of sheer terror.

We believe that most leaders experience that profound dichotomy every day, and it's a heavy burden. How many times have you feigned confidence to superiors or reports when you were really unsure? Have you ever felt comfortable conceding that you were confused by the latest business results or caught off guard by a competitor's move? Would you ever admit to feeling inadequate to cope with the complex issues your firm was facing? Anyone who can identify with these situations knows firsthand what it's like to be trapped in the myth of the complete leader—the person at the top without flaws. It's time to put that myth to rest, not only for the sake of frustrated leaders but also for the health of organizations. Even the most talented leaders require the input and leadership of others, constructively solicited and creatively applied. It's time to celebrate the incomplete—that is, the human—leader.

Originally published in February 2007. Reprint R0702E

About the Contributors

DEBORAH ANCONA is the Seley Distinguished Professor of Management at MIT's Sloan School of Management.

WARREN G. BENNIS is University Professor at the University of Southern California.

JIM COLLINS operates a management research laboratory in Boulder, Colorado.

PETER F. DRUCKER was a professor of social science and management at Claremont Graduate University in California.

BILL GEORGE is a professor of management practice at Harvard Business School.

DANIEL GOLEMAN cochairs the Consortium for Research on Emotional Intelligence in Organizations at Rutgers University.

ROBERT GOFFEE is a professor of organizational behavior at London Business School.

RONALD A. HEIFETZ codirects the Center for Public Leadership at Harvard University's Kennedy School of Government.

GARETH JONES is a fellow of the Centre for Management Development at London Business School.

JOHN P. KOTTER is the Konosuke Matsushita Professor of Leadership, Emeritus, at Harvard Business School.

DONALD L. LAURIE is a founder and managing partner at Oyster International, a Boston-based consulting firm.

THOMAS W. MALONE is the Patrick J. McGovern Professor of Management at MIT's Sloan School of Management.

DIANA MAYER is a former Citigroup executive in New York.

ANDREW N. McLEAN is a research associate at Harvard Business School.

WANDA J. ORLIKOWSKI is the Eaton-Peabody Professor of Communication Sciences at MIT's Sloan School of Management.

DAVID ROOKE is a director at Harthill Consulting in Hewelsfield, England.

PETER M. SENGE is a senior lecturer at MIT's Sloan School of Management.

PETER SIMS established "Leadership Perspectives," a class at the Stanford Graduate School of Business in California.

ROBERT J. THOMAS is a visiting professor of leadership at the Fletcher School of Law and Diplomacy at Tufts University.

WILLIAM R. TORBERT is a professor emeritus of leadership at the Carroll School of Management at Boston College.

Index

bonding, 106–107
Both, Hennie, 73, 74
bottom-line results, 177
BP (British Petroleum), 82, 93
brain, limbic system and neocortex of, 8
Branson, Richard, 83
breakthroughs, 125
British Airways, 2, 60, 62–64
British Petroleum. *See* BP
building support team, 173–175
buildup-breakthrough flywheel, 119, 124–125
bureaucracies, 84–85
businesses
  family-owned or family-run, 27–28
  linking to student-driven education, 100
business-process-reengineering and restructuring initiatives, 77
BusinessWeek, 126
BusinessWeek Online, 191

Cain, George, 128–129
Calvin Klein Cosmetics, 90
candor, 10, 11
capabilities, 2–3
capitalizing on uniqueness, 81–82
Car Launch (Roth and Kleiner), 192
Carlzon, Jan, 43, 66, 68–69
Carter, Jimmy, 99
CERES Environmental Principles, 149
challenges, adaptive, 57–58
change
  context for, 60
  coping with, 38–39, 41, 49, 52
  difficulty adjusting to rapid, 48
  Diplomats and, 143
  making happen, 58
  as opportunity, 32
  understanding of pain of, 66

charisma, 39
Charles Schwab, 168
check-in points, 26
Chrysler, 127–128
Ciba-Geigy, 167
Circuit City, 131–132
Citibank, 184
clarifying assumptions, 61
coaching, 18
Coca-Cola, 112, 115
cognitive abilities, 2
cognitive skills, 3
Cold War, 85
Coleman, Jack, 101, 111–112
collaboration, 61
  demonstrating need for, 67
  Experts and, 146
collaborative atmosphere, 81
collaborators, 19
collective self-confidence, 69
Collins, Jim, 117
commitment to organization, 15
Common Cause, 111
communicating, responsibility for, 26, 31–32
Communist China, 106–109
companies
  adaptive challenges, 57–58
  buildup-breakthrough flywheel, 124–125
  culture of discipline, 125
  failure to become great, 120
  good becoming great, 120–123
  Hedgehog concept, 125
  multiple factors for greatness, 124–125
  people first, 124
  Stockdale paradox, 124
  strategy second, 124
  technology accelerators, 125
compelling modesty, 126–128
competency models, 2

Smart advice and inspiration from a source you trust.